THE SONSHIP OF CHRIST

TY GIBSON

EXPLORING THE COVENANT IDENTITY OF GOD AND MAN

For Sue
Every beautiful thing I believe is informed by you

And for Jason, My Only Begotten Son
Being your father is always fun and sometimes dangerous

CONTENTS

"Daughters of Eve,
after all you've been
through, I want you to
know you were in my
thoughts every sentence
along the way."

KIDS KNOW STUFF

This book was written purely by accident.

No kidding.

It seems to have written itself. Yes, I was involved in the process, painfully so at times. But my next book was going to be about something else. In midstream, I got diverted, then obsessed, then overwhelmed by an unexpected vision of God's beauty, and I had to follow the light wherever it might lead. There were so many people asking the same basic question—people in Germany and Australia, Spain and California, and at the Village Market in Collegedale, Tennessee—that I started composing notes and answering emails, until, next thing I knew, this book popped out of my computer.

So here it is.

THE SONSHIP OF CHRIST
Exploring the Covenant Identity of God and Man

Admittedly, it's not a super catchy title, but it is very specific to the content of the book. So I'm hoping the title, and the subtitle, will become extremely meaningful to you before our journey's end. As I chased the thread woven through the pages ahead, before I knew it more than 100,000 words had been written. "Yikes! Stop already," I said to myself. So I stopped, and I edited. I didn't want to bury or bore you, so I cut the thing down to 43,459 words. That's manageable. In fact, at an average reading speed of 200 words per minute, you can get through this little volume in about three and a half hours. No sweat. That's a lazy Sunday afternoon, and I am confident it will be well worth your time.

Another thing about the title: yes, I am aware, extremely so, that "Sonship" is a *boy* word.

Daughters of Eve, after all you've been through, I want you to know you were in my thoughts every sentence along the way. Please keep in mind throughout this exploration that everything of which we speak regarding sons is equally applicable to daughters. Throughout the biblical narrative, Sonship is a covenant mechanism for tracing the lineage of Christ. Point is, my dear sisters, you are not excluded from any of the glorious implications of the biblical Sonship theme any more than men are excluded from the biblical portrayals of God's church as a woman and ultimately as a bride. Men along with women are represented by the bride, and women as well as men are represented by Sonship.

I'm so excited about *The Sonship of Christ* that I can't wait for you to read it. Please email me at hello@thesonshipofchrist.com and let me know what you think. I am praying, just so you know, that the ideas you are about to encounter will blow your mind and take you to a whole new level of biblical comprehension.

Finally, since books are expected to have introductions, here's mine:

Children tend to know more than adults—not more in mass, but more in meaning. As we grow older and "smarter" we tend to forget profound things nobody ever had to tell us. So this book is a wink and a nod to a little boy who intuitively sensed the essential make up of reality when he asked the rather brilliant question, "If we was created, well, that must mean God was alone before we was here, so how could God be nice way back then if there weren't nobody to be nice to? Maybe God weren't never alone."

Precisely, little guy.

"The Son of God cannot
be God in the same
eternal sense that
the Father is God, we
reason, or else He would
not be called the Son."

CHAPTER ONE

TWO IDENTITIES

What does the Bible mean when it calls Jesus "the Son of God"?

Oh, no! Is this gonna be one those boring, hairsplitting theological exercises?

Actually, no.

In fact, if you will take this little journey with me to its end, I assure you the rewards will be rich. You may even find yourself deeply moved by the beauty of God's character and awestruck by the utter genius of the biblical narrative. Even if you find the above question boring at first glance, I promise you our time together will not be boring in the least.

First of all, you should be aware that this question has challenged Bible students for nearly two thousand years. It's not an easy nut to crack. Scholars have been endlessly intrigued and baffled by the topic. And it's easy to see why. On the rather compelling premise that Scripture calls Christ "the Son of God," various groups have arisen throughout church history insisting that He could not, while bearing a title like that, preexist without a point of beginning, nor could He eternally coexist alongside the God whose "Son" He is. Logic, they insist, precludes a *son* from chronologically coexisting concurrent with a *father*.

You can hardly blame them.

Our normal understanding of "son" includes the idea of birth, and Jesus is said in Scripture to be "begotten" or birthed. Naturally, then, to be a "son" suggests a point of origin and a point of beginning. Since Jesus is called God's "Son," doesn't it follow that He must have been generated from God and, therefore, had a starting point as a distinct person from the Father?

Certainly, there is logic to the perspective.

So I want to say to those who take this view, you will find no disrespectful or dismissive attitude from me. I affirm you for being studious and for using your brain. As Galileo once said, "I do not feel obliged to believe that the same God who has endowed us with sense, reason, and intellect has intended us to forgo their use." You have simply attempted to be logical and consistent, and I commend you for that.

But on the premise of your honesty and logic, I am asking that you take a serious look at what we will explore on the topic, because I think you will find the perspective in this book to be profoundly convincing. I will make the bold claim, in fact, that what we are about to discover is so obviously the truth regarding the Sonship of Christ, that once you see it, you won't be able to unsee it. I realize this is a lot for this little book to live up to, but please allow me to give it my best shot by taking the journey with me to the last page. And whatever you do, do not jump ahead. Take the material in its order, because, in our treatment of the topic, one piece of the picture is vital to the next, and the next, and so on, to the end.

No matter who you are or what position you have taken on the Sonship of Christ, you have no doubt felt the tension and complexity involved in trying to make sense out of two apparently contradictory claims in Scripture.

On the one hand, the Bible calls Jesus God's "only begotten Son" (John 3:16) and describes Him as occupying a subordinate position under the Father (John 14:28; 1 Corinthians 15:27-28).

On the other hand, Scripture also states that Jesus is "in very nature God," insisting that He shares "equality with God" (Philippians 2:5-6) and that He is the One who "made" all things that are "made," placing Him, by contrast, in the *un*made category (John 1:1-3). He is even called "the everlasting Father" (Isaiah 9:6, KJV), the eternal "I AM" (Exodus 3:14; John 8:58), and "the Almighty" (Revelation 1:8).

The tension between the two identities is immediately apparent.

The solution needs to be consistent with both of these claims . . .

and worthy of our wonder.

"Most Christians have been taught to handle Scripture as a doctrinal textbook, with the assumption that it basically operates like an encyclopedia from which to compose a collection of theological propositions."

CHAPTER TWO

READING SCRIPTURE ON ITS OWN TERMS

I'm going to suggest that the reason we struggle to make sense of the Sonship of Christ is due to a selective and narrow reading of Scripture that ignores the overall storyline of the book. Not that anyone intends to read the Bible selectively or with a narrow focus. It's just that most Christians have been taught to handle Scripture as a doctrinal textbook, with the assumption that it basically operates like an encyclopedia from which to compose a collection of theological propositions. So we don't really read the Bible, per se, but rather we tend to comb its pages searching for verses, sentences, even partial sentences and isolated words, and we then assemble the disjointed mass of "verses" into topical categories from which we compose "beliefs."

The Bible writers themselves seem to know nothing of this topical framing of truth. It is apparently foreign to the ancient Hebrew way of processing reality. They, by contrast, see and convey the truth in the form of poetry and song, symbol and story—mostly story, since even the poems, songs, and symbols are enlisted to tell the story.

When the Bible is studied in a prooftext manner that overlooks context, it is possible, of course, to harness its many "verses" to formulate just about any "doctrine" a person is inclined to believe. Bible study, with this approach, is a rather subjective exercise in which I look for "verses" to support a premise that I usually bring to the Bible—and, no surprise, I find the support I'm looking for.

Using the prooftext approach to Scripture, we can easily, and with good intention, take hold of the word "son" as it occurs in reference to Jesus and then proceed to reason, quite apart from the biblical narrative, that He must have emerged from God sometime, long, long ago. The "Son of God" cannot be God in the same eternal sense that the "Father" is, we reason, or else He would not be called "the Son."

Then, in order to deal with the other "verses" that present Jesus as God, we are obliged to venture into more philosophical, abstract explanations that Scripture itself does not offer. We say things along the line of, "Yes, Jesus always existed *in* the Father before He was brought forth *from* the Father, so He wasn't *created by* the Father, but rather *emerged from* the Father." And we feel like we've said something meaningful and deep, although we don't really have any idea what we've said and we know the Bible, of course, says no such thing. But when we use a prooftext method that is not careful to notice context, we have no choice but to fill in the gaps with speculations that are not inherent to the text. In other words, we have to make stuff up.

Of course, we can't blame people for trying to make sense of difficult language. Operating within the prooftext methodology, focusing on a few trees while failing to see the whole forest, it really is quite challenging to make heads or tails out of "God" being "begotten" as "God's Son." So we either downplay or over interpret the verses that don't fit. Those who take the opposing view generally respond by assembling their own list of verses and offering their own strained interpretations. So we end up stranded on a prooftext impasse, my chosen texts against yours and yours against mine.

But there is a solution, and it is very clearly seen to be *the* solution once we engage with it and see where it leads:

Read the Bible.

The whole thing.

On its own terms.

When we read the Bible as an unfolding narrative—as the big story it actually is—with key characters played out in an overarching, intentional plot line, the meaning of the Sonship of Christ becomes unmistakably evident. In other words, if we really want to understand the sense in which Jesus is the Son of God, we need to pan out from our selected verses to take in the grand historical tale the prophets are telling.

When in doubt, pan out.

And when we do that—wow!—a whole new world of biblical understanding opens before us, and there is no need for strained interpretations. We just see it. The story tells us the truth in ways that micromanaging individual verses never can.

So let's do just that. Let's read the Bible on its own terms and see where it leads.

This is going to be exciting.

"When we use a prooftext method that is not careful to notice context, we have no choice but to fill in the gaps with speculations that are not inherent to the text. In other words, we have to make stuff up."

CHAPTER THREE

A PROPHECY OF PROGENY

The biblical story opens with God creating Adam and Eve.

They are the first human beings.

All other humans come from them.

There is an immediately evident pattern to the narrative: creation, procreation.

God created Adam and Eve in God's "own image" and then Adam, with no small amount of help from Eve, "begot a son in his own likeness, after his image" (Genesis 1:27; Genesis 5:3).

And this Adam fella, well, he is the first "son of God" in the biblical narrative, and he's the initial character in the story that gives meaning to the Sonship identity that is woven throughout the rest of the Bible. When we skip forward in the narrative to the New Testament, the deliberate intent of the "son" theme becomes evident. In Luke's genealogy of Jesus, each person in the lineage is called the "son" of some human father, until we get all the way back to Adam, the first man, who is distinguished from all the others like this:

> . . . Adam, the son of God. Luke 3:38

Do you see what just happened? The New Testament deliberately loops all the way back to the opening of the biblical story in order to tell us who Jesus is, and it does so by telling us who Adam was. There's Adam, and there's Jesus. And these two figures constitute the premise of the entire biblical story, as we will see with greater and greater clarity as we proceed.

From the outset of the story, God has a "son," and his name is Adam. God has a daughter, too, and she forms a vital thread of the story, as well, which will soon become evident. For now, we are interested in tracing the biblical thread of "son" in order to comprehend the Sonship of Jesus.

According to Luke, Adam is the "the son of God" in a more foundational sense than any of the human beings that follow him.

Why?

Well, quite simply because he is the first of his kind, the first human, from whom all others will emerge and receive their identity.

Adam and Eve were *created*.

Everyone else was *procreated*.

That's how the biblical story begins.

Adam was the head of the human race, from whom all of humanity would receive their "likeness." Beginning with him, the "image" of God was to be passed on from generation to generation, creating an ever-widening circle of human beings with the capacity to love like God loves, living in God's "image" or "likeness." That was the divine plan in humanity's creation. There was to be a succession of sons and daughters who would pass on God's image. Again, for clarity:

God created Adam and Eve in God's "own image" (Genesis 1:27).

Then Adam "begot a son in his own likeness, after his image" (Genesis 5:3).

What a wonderful plan!

But right here the story makes a tragic shift. An *interruption* was imposed upon the plan:

- an interruption we call the Fall of humanity

- an interruption in which the fallen angel, Lucifer, deceived humanity into believing God is arbitrary, restrictive, untrustworthy, and self-serving (Genesis 3:1-5)

- an interruption that nearly effaced the "image" of God from "the son of God," thus disrupting the capacity of God's son to transmit God's image from generation to generation

And because there was an interruption, an *intervention* was needed:

- an intervention that would have to happen from the *inside* of the human situation

- an intervention that would offer a new way forward with a new starting point

- an intervention that would come in the form of a new "Son of God" to replace Adam, a new head of the human race who would reestablish God's "image" in humanity

Directly after the Fall, the Creator issued a prophecy in the form of a threat to Satan and a promise to humanity:

> I will put enmity between you (Satan) and the woman (Eve and her progeny), and between your offspring and hers; He (the coming offspring) will crush your head, and you will strike His heel. Genesis 3:15, NIV

Don't miss the point.

The promise of deliverance is set forth in the language of *progeny* or *offspring*. Two groups of people will be at odds down through history. A spiritual lineage will issue forth from Satan, waging war against God and His people, while a spiritual lineage will issue forth from the woman, through which a special "offspring" will one day be born to conquer Satan and reverse the effects of the Fall. Adam, "the son of God," failed in the face of temptation, in his encounter with Satan. But a new Son will be born to the fallen race, and He will crush the serpent rather than yield to him. A second "Adam," a new "Son of God," will take the stage of human history and succeed where the first Adam failed.

We see, then, that from the outset of the story God is addressing the sin problem in terms of family succession, promising the eventual birth of a child. The God who made humanity intends to save humanity from the *inside*, from within our very own genetic realm, from the strategic position of a "Son of God" who will be born within Adam's lineage in order to redeem Adam's fall.

Once we have this initial piece of the biblical storyline clearly established in our minds, everything else along the way begins to make sense with profound clarity.

This is about to get really good. I'll be waiting for you in the next chapter.

"When we read the Bible as an unfolding narrative—as the big story it actually is—with key characters played out in an overarching, intentional plot line, the meaning of the Sonship of Christ becomes unmistakably evident."

CHAPTER FOUR

ISRAEL, MY SON

Already, the story has a distinct shape and we are beginning to see where it's going. With the first prophetic promise of Genesis 3:15 before us, the stage is set for the grand narrative arc of Scripture to unfold. What God does next is not surprising at all, given the key features of the story's first episode. He proceeds, of course, to take the steps necessary for the fulfillment of the promise.

And how does He do this?

Well, exactly as we would expect now that we are tuned into the story: by establishing a genealogical line through which the promised child, the new Son of God, may be born to the world.

So God calls Abraham and his wife Sarah out of Ur, their Babylonian homeland, and promises to establish a great nation within their genetic line, through which all the nations of the earth will be blessed (Genesis 12). God calls the promise His "covenant" (Genesis 15), and it is clearly an expanded version of the promise given in Genesis 3. Covenant emerges to view as the defining characteristic of the divine operation as the progeny plan moves forward, just as God vowed it would. So we are not at all surprised when Abraham and Sarah eventually give birth to Isaac and he is identified in Scripture as the "son" of "promise" (Genesis 21:1-7; Galatians 4:23).

It is crucial to notice that the story now begins to center on a succession of sons. At this point, the concept of primogeniture emerges in the narrative—the birthright of the "firstborn" son (Genesis 27:19, 32; 43:33; 48:14-18). The firstborn son is the channel through which the covenant promise is to be passed on from generation to generation. But—and this is hugely significant—in a narrative twist that emphasizes the spiritual nature of the plan, we soon see that the *genetic* firstborn isn't always the *covenant* firstborn.

Isaac is the second born son of Abraham, after Ishmael, but Isaac is the firstborn son of promise.

Isaac then marries Rebekah and the promise passes to their son, Jacob, who is the second born son, after Esau, and yet he occupies the covenant position of the firstborn son.

The underlying goal God is pursuing is the transmission of the covenant promise. God is not fixated on exact birth order, but rather on moving the covenant promise forward. What matters is that a line is established through which the new "Son of God" may enter the human situation and conquer the serpent from the inside, from the strategic position of human nature, thus reversing Adam's fall in the course of the victory.

The storyline unfolds toward its grand end goal, in brief, like this:

Abraham and Sarah have a firstborn covenant son they name Isaac.

Isaac and Rebekah have a firstborn covenant son they name Jacob.

Jacob's wives bring forth twelve sons. Jacob's name is changed to Israel. Then, oddly—or not so oddly within the overarching narrative—Jacob's twelve sons and all their children become known corporately by the covenant name of their father, Israel. God now has a corporate people, a nation. Israel then goes into Egypt and becomes an enslaved people. God eventually sends Moses to deliver Israel from Egyptian bondage, and—pay attention now—God instructs him to tell Pharaoh something rather specific:

> Israel is My son, My firstborn. So I say to you, let
> My son go that he may serve Me. Exodus 4:22-23

Israel, the nation, is now designated as God's "firstborn son," singular. At this point in the story, the progeny language initiated in Genesis 3:15 takes on an expanded application of corporate Sonship with regards to Israel as a nation. In what sense is Israel God's firstborn son? The answer is evident when we recall the promise to Abraham:

> In you, all the families of the earth shall be
> blessed. Genesis 12:3

Israel is God's firstborn *nation*-son with the intent that, through the witness of Israel, many other nations will become *nation*-sons of God, as well. Again, we see that

the position or role of the "firstborn son" has nothing
to do with birth order. It has to do with the conveyance
of the covenant to all the nations of the earth. Israel is
the spiritual channel through which God intends to
incorporate all nations into the Sonship status that was
lost by Adam. Isaac, Jacob, and then Israel, were all
"firstborn" in a *positional* sense or in a *functional* sense,
not in a *chronological* sense.

It is at this point in the biblical narrative—when Israel is
designated as God's firstborn son—that God assumes the
role of "Father" in relation to Israel. Rebuking Israel for
their unfaithfulness to God, Moses said,

> Is He not your Father, who bought you?
> Has He not made you and established you? . . .
>
> They provoked Him to jealousy with foreign gods;
> With abominations they provoked Him to anger.
>
> They sacrificed to demons, not to God,
> To gods they did not know,
> To new gods, new arrivals,
> That your fathers did not fear.
>
> Of the Rock who begot you, you are unmindful,
> And have forgotten the God who fathered you.
> Deuteronomy 32:6, 16-18

Moses tells Israel:

God is "your Father."

God "begot you."

God "fathered you."

Now, with Israel taking on the role of God's only begotten son among the nations, God takes on the role of Father to Israel. For the first time in the biblical narrative, God now employs the language of birthing. He "begot" Israel as His chosen people among the nations. Israel, as God's only begotten son among the nations, is chastised because he has "forgotten the God who fathered" him, a fathering and birthing that occurred when God delivered Israel from Egyptian bondage. Israel was turning to the "gods" of the other nations and thus denying the God who fathered him. As God would later say through Jeremiah, "I am a Father to Israel, and Ephraim is My firstborn" (Jeremiah 31:9). The other nations are under the authority of their demon gods (Deuteronomy 32:17), but Israel is God's chosen people, called out from among the nations to be God's only begotten son, through whom all the other nations will be blessed.

As with the Sonship role, the fatherhood of God is grounded in the Old Testament narrative and is tightly connected with Israel's calling as the people through which the Messiah will enter the world. If we want to understand what the New Testament means when it calls God "Father," we must allow the story itself to tell us what it means. When we do that—when we think in theological obedience to the narrative of the Bible—it becomes evident that there is a sense in which God is our Father and the Father of Jesus, and there is a sense in which God cannot ultimately be confined to fatherhood, which we will explore later in this study.

A consistent picture is building as we simply follow the biblical narrative where it leads. We're on the edge of our seats at this point as the implications of Sonship begin to form in our minds. By letting the story itself guide us, we are about to understand the Bible on a whole new level. It only gets more astounding from here, so watch, ever so carefully, what happens next.

"There's Adam, and there's Jesus. And these two figures constitute the premise of the entire biblical story."

CHAPTER FIVE

DAVID, MY SON

Israel, God's "firstborn son," now liberated from bondage, grows as a nation, generation after generation, until a boy named David is born.

You may have heard David's story as an isolated inspirational tale with cute lessons about conquering personal "giants" that stand against your professional success (Goliath) with your five personality strengths (your five smooth stones), but it's more than that. David's story is, quite profoundly, the seamless continuation of the Bible's big covenant narrative.

David is, in fact, the next son of God in Scripture's Sonship saga.

He becomes the chosen king of Israel and, in him, Israel's corporate identity is now represented. The Sonship identity now takes on a more detailed prophetic significance. The birth order ideal is upset, yet again, because David is not the firstborn son of his father, Jesse, but rather the last-born (1 Samuel 16:10-11).

Again, it is the historical continuance of the covenant that matters, not chronological birth order. With David God reaffirms the covenant promise He made to Abraham, Isaac, Jacob, and Israel, and David then becomes an expanded prototype of the coming Messiah.

Watch this.

In order to convey the idea of succession, Scripture again invokes the language of "son." In Psalm 2:1-7, David sings of himself being "begotten" as God's "son," while simultaneously singing prophetically of the coming Messiah, in whom all God has promised to the world through Israel will be fulfilled:

> Why do the nations rage,
> and the people plot a vain thing?
>
> The kings of the earth set themselves,
> and the rulers take counsel together,
> against the Lord and against His Anointed
> (*Messiah* in Hebrew) . . .
>
> Yet I have set My King on My holy hill of Zion.
>
> I will declare the decree: the Lord has said to Me,
> "You are My Son, today I have begotten You."

Who is David singing about?

Well, he is singing about himself in the immediate, local historical sense. David is the anointed king of Israel. But he is also singing prophetically about the ultimate, universal anointed king of Israel, namely Jesus Christ. We know this to be the case because the New Testament makes this prophetic connection (Acts 2:25-36; Acts 4:25-28; Acts 13:33; Hebrews 1:5).

In Psalm 89:19-29, David portrays himself as God's
"firstborn" son through whom His "covenant shall stand
firm," while again foretelling the coming of the Messiah:

> Then You spoke in a vision to Your holy one,
> And said: "I have given help to one who is mighty;
> I have exalted one chosen from the people.
>
> "I have found My servant David;
> With My holy oil I have anointed him,
> With whom My hand shall be established;
> Also My arm shall strengthen him.
>
> "The enemy shall not outwit him,
> Nor the son of wickedness afflict him.
>
> "I will beat down his foes before his face,
> And plague those who hate him.
>
> "But My faithfulness and My mercy shall
> be with him,
> And in My name his horn shall be exalted.
>
> "Also I will set his hand over the sea,
> And his right hand over the rivers.
>
> "He shall cry to Me, 'You are my Father,
> My God, and the rock of my salvation.'

"Also I will make him My firstborn,
The highest of the kings of the earth.

"My mercy I will keep for him forever,
And My covenant shall stand firm with him.

"His seed also I will make to endure forever,
And his throne as the days of heaven."

Again, we naturally ask, of whom is David singing?

Who is the holy one?

Who is the exalted one chosen from the people?

Who is the one who cries out, "You are my Father," to whom God responds, "I will make him My firstborn"?

Who is the highest king of the earth, in whom God's covenant will be established forever?

David, of course, and yet more than David!

At this point in our journey, knowing what we know, simply reading these two Psalms of David should flip a light on in our minds. These Old Testament passages are vital for grasping the story as it continues into the New Testament, specifically regarding what the New Testament means when it calls Jesus God's "firstborn son" and God's "only begotten son." These psalms of David are the origin of the terminology, along with the earlier passages we've noted regarding Israel's Sonship. In fact, as we will discover, the New Testament specifically quotes these two Psalms to inform us of the covenant identity of the Messiah.

Therefore—and this is crucial—it is here in the Old Testament narrative that we need to look to interpret the terminology of Sonship when we encounter it in the New Testament.

And we will do just that, shortly.

For now, we simply need to notice, in the interest of our future enlightenment, that David portrays himself, as well as the coming Messiah, as "begotten" by God and as God's "firstborn son," not in a literal chronological sense, but in a positional, narrative sense. David is God's covenant son in a succession of sons, all leading up to the messianic Son who will cry out to God, with a newly realized Sonship fidelity, "You are my Father." And He is the One who will "endure forever."

The point is simple, but super important: King David does not step onto the biblical stage in a narrative vacuum. He emerges in the middle of an unfolding saga. Adam, the son of God, forfeited his Sonship position. God promised to get it back by giving the human race a new Genesis with a new Son of God who will succeed where Adam failed. The coming offspring of the woman will faithfully occupy

His vocation as the eternal progenitor of God's image to all future generations.

The internal logic of the biblical narrative is consistent. God is working to restore humanity from the inside, from within our own genetic realm, through a human Son of God who will rectify the fall of Adam. David is one more step in the Sonship succession.

So what's next?

You guessed it—another son of God.

"The God who made humanity intends to save humanity from the inside, from within our very own genetic realm, from the strategic position of a Son of God who will be born within the Adamic lineage."

CHAPTER SIX
SOLOMON, MY SON

As the story continues to unfold, David has a son, to whom he gives the name Solomon. True to the trajectory of the plan, God transfers to Solomon the unique position of Sonship:

> He shall build a house for My name, and he shall be My son, and I will be his Father; and I will establish the throne of his kingdom over Israel forever. 1 Chronicles 22:10

Note the language carefully, because it re-emerges in the New Testament: "He *shall be* My son, and I *will be* his Father." Not, He *is* my son, and *I am* his Father. These are narrative roles that are being occupied for a covenant purpose. Solomon is conscripted into the Sonship position for the continuation of the covenant plan.

Solomon is significant in the lineage because his story, unlike that of his father, David, unfolds without war. David, the son of God, expresses a desire to build a temple for the worship of God, but He explains to him that he cannot be the one to build God's temple (2 Samuel 7).

Why?

Well, because David is a man of war with blood on his hands (1 Chronicles 17, 22, 28). Within the biblical narrative, God's character is ultimately incompatible with war (Isaiah 2:1-4), so a man of peace must build God's temple. That man is Solomon, whose name means *peace*—peace from war, that is (1 Chronicles 22:9). In this way, as the covenant promise is transferred from David to Solomon, God is projecting forward to the grander purpose He will eventually achieve through Christ. In a penultimate sense, Solomon is God's peaceful son, pointing forward to Jesus, the ultimate Prince of Peace. He is the One in whom God will "establish the throne of His kingdom over Israel forever," without war.

So with Solomon, we are one step closer, or one "son of God" closer, to the promised Messiah. The story has a very distinct, obvious shape.

Adam, the son of God, fails in his Sonship role.

God promises to initiate a lineage through which a new Son of God will come to rectify Adam's fall.

God establishes a people through whom the promise will be fulfilled, and a succession unfolds in the following manner:

Abraham, the son of God, gives way to . . .

Isaac, the son of God, who gives way to . . .

Jacob, the son of God, who gives way to . . .

Israel, the corporate son of God, who gives way to . . .

David, the son of God, who gives way to . . .

Solomon, the son of God.

Clarity is building. Scripture is a seamless narrative. The story is initiated with the creation of the first man and the first woman, Adam and Eve, and then makes its way forward through the call of Abraham, the establishment of Israel, the anointing of David as Israel's king, then to Solomon, the king of peace, all moving to one grand end:

- the birth of the promised offspring,

- an Adamic replacement who will redeem the Fall,

- a human being who will be "the son of God" with covenantal faithfulness and thus reestablish humanity in right relation to God.

"Human history
is fundamentally
characterized by
covenant breaking. We
are a race defined by
relational dysfunction
and disintegration,
a race of victims and
victimizers, a race
of non-lovers."

CHAPTER SEVEN

COVENANT IDENTITY

Before we cross the bridge from the Old Testament into the New—from shadowy messianic figures to the Messiah Himself—let's pause to achieve a clear grasp of what the Bible means by the idea of "covenant," because this is the theological engine that drives the biblical story forward, as we've already noticed.

For its sheer conceptual worth, "covenant" is one of the most meaningful words in Scripture. It is *the* idea that most fully defines who God is and how God operates. God is a God of covenant, actuated by covenant, only and always living within the dynamic relational flow of covenant.

So what does this heavily freighted word mean?

Speaking through the prophet Hosea, God reveals His heart for Israel and all of humanity in covenant terms:

> For I desire steadfast love and not sacrifice, the knowledge of God rather than burnt offerings. But like Adam they transgressed the covenant; there they dealt faithlessly with Me. Hosea 6:6-7, ESV

First, notice that the "covenant" entails "steadfast love." Notice also that the Fall of Adam and, by extension, the fallen state of humanity as a whole, is defined with the words, "they transgressed the covenant." Clearly, then, "covenant" encompasses the entire biblical narrative, reaching back to God's original purpose for humanity,

and reaching forward to God's ultimate "desire" for
the world.

Speaking through the prophet Isaiah, God expressed the
essence of His covenant like this:

> "Though the mountains be shaken
> and the hills be removed,
> yet my unfailing love for you will not be shaken,
> nor my covenant of peace be removed,"
> says the Lord, who has compassion on you.
> Isaiah 54:10, NIV

> Give ear and come to me;
> listen, that you may live.

> I will make an everlasting covenant with you,
> my faithful love promised to David.
> Isaiah 55:3, NIV

Wow, so beautiful, and so rich with relational significance!

Here, again, we see that covenant is a relational dynamic
that involves:

- steadfast love

- unfailing love

- faithful love

Or we could say it like this: covenant involves living with unbreakable relational integrity. To say that God is a God of covenant, is to say that God is relationally faithful to all others above and before Himself, and at any and all cost to Himself. Covenant is, therefore, a biblical word that communicates God's core identity, His essential character. To the question, Who is God?, the Bible answers, God is covenantally faithful!

But covenant does not merely reveal who God is, it also reveals what it really means to be human. In the Hosea 6 passage, the God of covenant desires only one thing from human beings: steadfast love or covenantal faithfulness. By logical contrast, covenant breaking defines what it looks like when humans are out of sync with their true identity. Watch how Isaiah articulates the idea:

> The earth is also defiled under its inhabitants,
> Because they have transgressed the laws,
> Changed the ordinance,
> Broken the everlasting covenant.
>
> Therefore the curse has devoured the earth,
> And those who dwell in it are desolate.
> Isaiah 24:5-6

Human history is fundamentally characterized by covenant breaking. We are a race defined by relational dysfunction and disintegration, a race of victims and victimizers, a race of *non*-lovers.

Covenant is a relational word. To live covenantally is to live for all others in faithful love. Covenant breaking occurs when individuals live for self to the hurt of others. According to Isaiah, our covenant breaking has adversely impacted the earth itself. The very ecosystem has been "defiled" and "devoured" by our violation of the earth's covenant system. In short, everything wrong with the world is due to broken covenant, which is to say, everything wrong with the world is due to broken relationships, or violated love. All God wants for the world is for covenant faithfulness to be restored as our fundamental mode of existing. God only desires that each one would care for the wellbeing of all the other ones.

Covenant, in a nutshell, is omni-directional love: love between God and humans, love between humans and humans, and love between humans and the creation over which they have charge.

But obviously, that's not what's going on in the world.

So God became human in order to live out the relational terms of the covenant *for* us, *toward* us, *in* us, and *as* us.

Through Isaiah, God said to the coming Messiah, "I, the Lord, have called You in righteousness, and will hold Your hand; I will keep You and give You as a covenant to the people, as a light to the Gentiles" (Isaiah 42:6). Then Daniel came along and foretold that the coming Messiah would "confirm the covenant" and be named "the

Prince of the covenant" (Daniel 9:27; 11:22, KJV). Finally, Malachi closed the Old Testament by calling the coming Messiah, "the Messenger of the covenant" (Malachi 3:1).

The Messiah is:

- God's covenant to the people in personified form

- God's steadfast love moving in all relational directions with perfect integrity

- God's covenantal faithfulness to the human race "confirmed"

In brief, Scripture is the story of God living in covenantal love *toward us* with the aim of restoring covenantal love *in us*. The plan of salvation is the historical process through which God keeps on loving us at any and all cost to Himself, reproducing the image of God in humanity by means of self-sacrifice (John 12:23-32). Jesus envisioned the final form of redeemed humanity in precisely these terms. He prayed "that the love with which You (Father) loved Me (the Son) may be in them, and I in them" (John 17:26). God's desire is that human beings would be reincorporated into the very love that flows freely between the Father and His only faithful covenant Son, Jesus Christ.

There is a core purpose embedded within the biblical narrative, and it is this:

God is seeking to complete the relational loop of covenantal faithfulness between Himself and the human race, to restore relational integrity within humanity so that the love flowing from Him to us might finally flow back to Him from us and outward to one another. Jesus is the Son of God through whom this purpose is created and procreated, actualized and then transmitted, achieved and then disseminated, produced and then reproduced.

If we understand this single idea, we understand the basic internal logic of the entire Bible. Every promise and prophecy, every story and song, every poem and parable of the book serves this grand narrative arc.

With that, we are now ready to step into the New Testament. Let's start with the big picture by taking in a brief sweeping glance, and then we will circle back around for more detailed considerations.

"Covenant, in a nutshell,
is omnidirectional
love: love between
God and humans,
love between humans
and humans, and love
between humans and
the creation over which
they have charge."

CHAPTER EIGHT

THE GRAND
REENACTMENT

A covenant was made, to which God was faithful and Israel was not. As the Son of God, the life of Jesus was a complete and faithful reenactment of Israel's history. It would not be an exaggeration to say that this is the whole point of the Bible.

Christ passed over the same experiential ground Israel traversed, but He was true to the covenant in place of Israel's failure. The parallels between the two stories are deliberate and striking, although most of us have never been taught to read Scripture in a manner that would allow us to notice the intentional narrative linkage between the Old Testament and the New. Some branches of Christianity have gone so far as to completely negate the Old Testament and discourage people from reading it. It is even popular to print the New Testament alone, placing in millions of people's hands only half of the book, thus making it virtually impossible for the reader to gain an accurate view of who Jesus was and why He came to our world.

Let's take a different approach. Let's pan way out and observe the seamless connection between the Old Testament and the New. In this chapter, let's take in the inspired artistry of the Bible by summarizing its story in the most minimalistic fashion we can.

In the Old Testament, a young man named Joseph had dreams and was sent into Egypt to preserve his family, followed by Israel, the nation, relocating to Egypt to escape certain death (Genesis 42; 45:5). In the New Testament, another Joseph had dreams and then fled with His family into Egypt to escape the certain death of Israel, now reborn in the Christ child (Matthew 2:13-15).

When Israel came out of Egypt, God called the nation, "my son" (Exodus 4:22). When Jesus came out of Egypt, God said, "Out of Egypt have I called my son" (Matthew 2:15), forging an intentional parallel between the story of ancient Israel and the story of Jesus as God's new Israelite son.

God's son, Israel, passed through the Red Sea as they fled from the Egyptian army (Exodus 14:10-13). The apostle Paul says they were thus "baptized unto Moses . . . in the sea" (1 Corinthians 10:2, KJV). Directly after being baptized as Israel's new corporate representative, Jesus was introduced to the world by God with the words, "This is My beloved Son, in whom I am well pleased" (Matthew 3:13-17). Jesus is relaunching Israel's history, this time to please God with covenantal faithfulness.

Israel wandered in the wilderness for 40 years on its way to the Promised Land, yielding to temptation over and over again, finally entering into Canaan under the leadership of a leader bearing the name, "Joshua," which means, *Yahweh Saves* (Exodus 16; Numbers 13). Christ spent 40 days in the wilderness being tempted by the devil without ever yielding, before He began His earthly ministry to lead humanity into the heavenly Promised

Land under the name "Jesus," which means *Yahweh Saves,* the Greek equivalent of *Joshua* (Matthew 1:21; 4:1-11).

Moses went up Mount Sinai to receive the Ten Commandments from God and then delivered them to Israel (Exodus 19-20). Jesus positioned Himself at another mountain in Israel, announcing that He had now come to "fulfill" the law, magnifying its relational significance, and pronouncing His blessings, or beatitudes, upon the people (Matthew 5-7).

Ancient Israel was composed of the twelve sons of Jacob and their posterity (Genesis 35:22-26). Jesus deliberately followed this narrative pattern by calling twelve apostles, from which emerged a spiritual posterity that would become the continuation of Israel, called the church, now composed of all nations (Matthew 10:1-4; Galatians 3:29; Ephesians 2:19-22).

Israel was called by God to be "a kingdom of priests, and an holy nation," for the purpose of being a light to all nations, the intent being to incorporate into Israel every people group of the world (Exodus 19:6; Deuteronomy 4:5-8, 40, KJV). The church Jesus founded was the new Israel, called to be "a chosen generation, a royal priesthood, an holy nation, a peculiar people" (1 Peter 2:9, KJV), composed of people from every nation (Revelation 7), and given the mission of bringing the light of God's love to the whole world (Matthew 24:14; 28:18-20; Revelation 14:6).

Wow, so all of that is there in the Bible, isn't it?

Yes, it sure is.

The sheer literary art of the narrative is so breathtaking that it simply cannot be a coincidental production. The chances of more than forty authors, writing over a span of fifteen hundred years, composing a seamless story of such pure genius, without the guidance of a single Super Mind, are so remote as to be impossible. But that's not even the most astounding part of it. The truly remarkable thing is that this story invites us to believe the very thing we secretly hope in our inmost hearts to be true—namely, that we are the objects of a faithful love that would rather die than let us go. One of the reasons we can know the story of Scripture is true is because it is true to our deepest longings for a quality of love that finds no perfectly satisfying match in this covenant-breaking world of ours. Jesus embodies what we intuitively know we are made for—perfect relational integrity.

And yet most Christians are never taught to even notice the deliberate narrative connection between the Old Testament and the New, let alone grasp what it means for the restoration of God's love in human relations. Our focus has largely been directed to egocentric concerns for personal salvation. The theological vision of Christianity became so thoroughly saturated in Greek thought by the medieval church, that the distinctly Hebrew orientation toward covenant relationship is almost unknown to modern Christianity.

The Bible is telling us a story. The goal of the story is that covenantal love would be restored to the human race. Jesus is the central, towering figure of the story. He is the one in whom the entire covenant enterprise is finally and fully achieved. In Christ, we witness the grand reenactment of Israel's history, this time with covenant faithfulness. In Him, everything God envisioned for Israel, and for the whole human race, has come true. In every act of His life, to the point of giving His life for his enemies as the climactic act of covenantal faithfulness, Jesus lived out God's love, and, in so doing, He fulfilled the entire Old Testament narrative with all of its covenant ideals and relational imperatives. Paul clearly understood this when he summarized the whole Bible in a single sentence:

> For all the promises of God in Him are Yes, and in Him Amen, to the glory of God through us.
> 2 Corinthians 1:20

The grand narrative arc of Scripture lands with colorful bursts of light and life in the person of Christ. Everything God promised to the world through Israel, God's unfaithful son, was now brought to pass in God's faithful Son, Jesus Christ. The story of Jesus is a microcosm of Israel's history, only this time the story is beautiful with unfailing love. This, then, is the sense in which the New Testament calls Jesus, "the Son of God."

Let's unpack the New Testament details now.

"The moment the big picture of the Bible dawns on us and we are theologically obedient to its storyline, we realize something startlingly simple that has been right under our noses all along."

CHAPTER NINE

MATTHEW'S GOSPEL—SON OF ABRAHAM

If we really want to understand what the Bible itself means when it speaks of Jesus as God's Son, we need to allow the New Testament to tells us the story of Jesus on its own terms, within its own framework, defining its own language. And it does just that if we will listen. With obvious intentionality, the New Testament opens by reaching into the past in order to coherently launch into the future:

> The book of the genealogy of Jesus Christ, the Son of David, the Son of Abraham . . . Matthew 1:1

Boom!

Boom?

Yes, boom!

I know, I know, we're all bored silly with the "genealogies," but that's only because we are floating adrift from the storyline of Scripture in favor of a more myopic approach in which we formulate propositional lists of detached doctrinal tenants. Systematic theology and sound doctrine are vitally important when conducted within the framework of the biblical narrative, but not as a methodology that quotes isolated Bible verses to formulate theological ideas that run contrary to the overall story of Scripture.

Recently somebody asked me, "If you could pull one massive practical joke on the worldwide church, what would it be?" I immediately responded, "I'd remove all the chapter and verse divisions from all the Bibles in the world."

Of course, that would be super funny, but my point was no joke at all. If we didn't have the chapter and verse divisions—which were imposed on Scripture rather recently in history—we'd be forced to read the actual story of the book. Many of us don't know what's really going on in the Bible, all the while living under the illusion that we have "the truth" simply because we have composed a prooftext arsenal of fundamental beliefs. Fundamental beliefs are important, but they mean little when held apart from their capacity for revealing the love of God as conveyed through the overall story of the Bible.

The Bible is the domain of narrative, not of propositional lists unmoored from narrative.

So the *truer* truth of Scripture belongs only to those who read the story and realize its centering and climax in Christ.

When we open the New Testament, the first thing we're told is that Jesus is none other than "the Son of David, the Son of Abraham." This should immediately alert us to the fact that we are about to pick up precisely where the story left off in the Old Testament. Part of the story is built into the names of these two key figures. Abraham means "father of many" and David means "beloved." The Messiah

who has now come in their lineage is God's "beloved
son," and He is here in our world to convey God's love to
the world and thus become "the father of many" more
beloved sons of God. After telling us that Jesus is "the
Son of David, the Son of Abraham," Matthew proceeds
to build his Gospel as the natural outworking of the Old
Testament narrative:

> And Jacob begot Joseph the husband of Mary, of
> whom was born Jesus who is called Christ. . . .
> Now the birth of Jesus Christ was as follows: After
> His mother Mary was betrothed to Joseph, before
> they came together, she was found with child of
> the Holy Spirit. Then Joseph her husband, being
> a just man, and not wanting to make her a public
> example, was minded to put her away secretly. But
> while he thought about these things, behold, an
> angel of the Lord appeared to him in a dream,
> saying, "Joseph, son of David, do not be afraid
> to take to you Mary your wife, for that which is
> conceived in her is of the Holy Spirit. And she
> will bring forth a Son, and you shall call His
> name Jesus, for He will save His people from
> their sins." So all this was done that it might be
> fulfilled which was spoken by the Lord through
> the prophet, saying: "Behold, the virgin shall be
> with child, and bear a Son, and they shall call His
> name Immanuel," which is translated, "God with
> us." Then Joseph, being aroused from sleep, did as
> the angel of the Lord commanded him and took

to him his wife, and did not know her till she had brought forth her firstborn Son. And he called His name Jesus. Matthew 1:16-25

Matthew wants his reader to understand that Jesus is the One Israel has been waiting for, the Christ (*Messiah*, in Hebrew). Look at his family lineage. Look at the miraculous circumstances of His birth, like what happened with Isaac, only this time the child is none other than "Immanuel," God in the flesh, just as Isaiah foretold. Look at the fact that the angel told His parents to name Him "Jesus" (*Joshua*, in Hebrew), after the successor of Moses who led Israel into the Promised Land. *Look, look, look,* Matthew is saying, making one connection after another between Jesus and the ancient story.

Jesus was born in Bethlehem, the city of David, because, after all, He is the son of David (Matthew 2:1-6).

With his parents, Jesus had to flee for survival to Egypt, but then later came out of Egypt, "that it might be fulfilled which was spoken by the Lord through the prophet, saying, 'Out of Egypt I called My Son'" (Matthew 2:13-15).

An Elijah-like figure, John the Baptist, announced and introduced Him, just as the prophet Isaiah said would happen (Isaiah 40). And then, when He was baptized by John, the voice of God came from heaven saying, "This is My beloved Son, in whom I am well pleased" (Matthew

3:17). The Son of God, the Son of David—same difference for Matthew, because he knows his Hebrew Bible.

Having come "out of Egypt," Jesus went "into the wilderness to be tempted by the devil . . . forty days and forty nights," just as ancient Israel went into the wilderness as God's "son" and was tempted by the devil for forty years (Matthew 4:1-2). Satan's attack on Jesus was aimed at questioning His Sonship identity. "If You are the Son of God," in the Israelite sense, "command that these stones become bread" (Matthew 4:3). Jesus is Israel in the wilderness all over again.

Having faced the devil in the wilderness and remained faithful to the covenant Israel failed to keep, Jesus immediately went about announcing, "Repent, for the kingdom of heaven is at hand" (Matthew 4:17). In other words, Jesus is proceeding to do precisely what ancient Israel was supposed to do—establishing the kingdom of God:

> Now, therefore, if you will indeed obey My voice and keep My covenant, then you shall be a special treasure to Me above all people; for all the earth is Mine. And you shall be to Me a kingdom of priests and a holy nation. Exodus 19:5-6

If Israel had been faithful to the covenant, God would have made them a great nation, and they would have become the attraction of the world:

See, I have taught you decrees and laws as
the Lord my God commanded me, so that you
may follow them in the land you are entering to
take possession of it. Observe them carefully, for
this will show your wisdom and understanding
to the nations, who will hear about all these
decrees and say, "Surely this great nation is a wise
and understanding people." What other nation
is so great as to have their gods near them the
way the Lord our God is near us whenever we
pray to him? And what other nation is so great
as to have such righteous decrees and laws as
this body of laws I am setting before you today?
Deuteronomy 4:5-8, NIV

All the nations of the world would have come to Israel
in order to learn of their good God. The principles of the
covenant would have given them success and they would
have flourished in every aspect of life. The kingdom of
God would have filled the whole world through Israel's
witness. But that never happened. So Matthew wants us
to understand that when Jesus comes announcing "the
kingdom of God," He is in the process of redeeming
Israel's failure to be God's faithful Son to the nations.

In order to set up the kingdom, Jesus proceeds to do two
things in Matthew's telling of the story:

1. He selects twelve apostles, mirroring the twelve sons of Jacob and the twelve tribes of Israel. According to Matthew, Jesus is founding a new Israel.

2. He embarks upon the mission Israel was supposed to execute—namely, to break down all ethnic barriers and incorporate the Gentiles into the covenant kingdom of God.

> And Jesus went about all Galilee, teaching in their synagogues, preaching the gospel of the kingdom, and healing all kinds of sickness and all kinds of disease among the people. Then His fame went throughout all Syria; and they brought to Him all sick people who were afflicted with various diseases and torments, and those who were demon-possessed, epileptics, and paralytics; and He healed them. Great multitudes followed Him—from Galilee, and from Decapolis, Jerusalem, Judea, and beyond the Jordan.
> Matthew 4:23-25

Israel's failed evangelistic mission is now being executed by Jesus, who is the faithful Son of God Israel was supposed to be. By telling us that Christ went about "healing all kinds of sickness," Matthew is reminding us of the covenant promise to Israel: "And I will take sickness away from the midst of you" (Exodus 23:25). "And the Lord will take away from you all sickness" (Deuteronomy 7:15). Step by step, act by act, Jesus is redeeming Israel's failed calling. As the realization regarding His messianic identity builds, "all the multitudes were amazed and said, 'Could this be the Son of David?'" (Matthew 12:23).

Matthew says, *Yes, yes, yes, that's exactly who He is!*

The whole purpose of Matthew's Gospel account is to persuade us that Jesus is the ultimate covenant Son of God to which all the penultimate covenant sons of God were pointing.

He is the Son of promise typified in Abraham's miracle-birth son, Isaac.

He is the covenant Son represented in Isaac's son, Jacob.

He is the firstborn Son of God foreshadowed in Jacob's sons, who collectively composed God's nation-son, Israel.

He is God's begotten and anointed Son, of which King David was a mere shadow.

He is the peaceful Son of God who came to establish God's eternal kingdom without war, prefigured in David's son, Solomon.

The moment the big picture of the Bible dawns on us and we are theologically obedient to its storyline, we realize something startlingly simple that has been right under our noses all along, and it is this:

Jesus is the Son of God in the sense that He fulfilled the entire narrative plot line of the Old Testament by successfully living out the purpose God had for humanity all along.

This. Is. The. Point. Of. The. Bible.

It is evident, then, and will become increasingly more evident as we proceed, that when the New Testament writers call Jesus "the Son of God," they are *not* trying to tell us anything about His ontological origins. They are *not* attempting to inform us about His metaphysical history. They are *not* aiming to educate us regarding how or when He came into existence way back in eternity past. Rather, they are telling us that Jesus is the son of promise in the Abrahamic, Davidic lineage. According to Matthew, Jesus is "the Son of David, the Son of Abraham," and, as such, He is the long-awaited Son of God who would be true to the covenant.

"The Fall of Adam
was the point of legal
transfer of earth into
Satan's control. In Christ
we have a new Adam
who has now arrived
on the scene to reverse
the effects of the Fall
and reclaim dominion
over the earth."

CHAPTER TEN

LUKE'S GOSPEL— SON OF ADAM

As with Matthew's Gospel, Luke's account is grounded in the narrative logic of the Old Testament:

> Then the angel said to her, "Do not be afraid, Mary, for you have found favor with God. And behold, you will conceive in your womb and bring forth a Son, and shall call His name Jesus. He will be great, and will be called the Son of the Highest; and the Lord God will give Him the throne of His father David. And He will reign over the house of Jacob forever, and of His kingdom there will be no end." Luke 1:30-33

Note the narrative indicators. Mary, the woman (think Genesis 3:15), brings forth a Son to occupy the throne of David and reign over the house of Jacob. Gabriel, the angel messenger, makes a point of explaining to Mary the Davidic identity of the child in her womb. He will "be called the Son of the Highest." It is a title He bears within the narrative of Scripture, according to Luke, not an explanation of His ancient origin. Luke is fully conscious of the story that is now reaching its climax in Christ. He wants us to understand that Jesus is God's Son in the same sense that David was, within the flow of God's covenant plan. Jesus is the One who fulfills the role that David and all the other sons of God failed to actualize. Unlike them, Jesus will be true to the original human calling. He will be faithful to the covenant of Sonship.

We have clarity, then, because we are now reading the New Testament in light of the Old. It is evident that Gabriel is not endeavoring to tell Mary that Jesus was begotten by God the Father way back in eternity past. That concern is nowhere on the angel's radar, nor anywhere on the radar of the biblical writers. The point Gabriel is communicating to Mary is that her child is the long-awaited "Son of God" who will live and reign as God's faithful Son on the throne of David.

Luke also wants us to know that Jesus, because He is the child of the covenant promise, came into the world by a miracle conception:

> Then Mary said to the angel, "How can this be, since I do not know a man?" And the angel answered and said to her, "The Holy Spirit will come upon you, and the power of the Highest will overshadow you; therefore, also, that Holy One who is to be born will be called the Son of God."
> Luke 1:34-35

Notice that He will "*therefore* . . . be *called* the Son God." It is a conferred title, a missional moniker in Luke's telling, not a description of His intrinsic, pre-incarnate identity. He will be *called* the Son of God precisely because He was conceived in Mary's womb by a miracle, as was Isaac, not because He always was the Son of God by nature before coming to our world. We will later explore that there is a sense in which Jesus was God's Son prior to His incarnation, but that discovery, too, will be grounded in the larger story Scripture is telling. For now, we are paying attention to what Luke is telling us. In the person of Jesus Christ, the long-awaited "Son of God" arrives, and to our complete astonishment, it is God Himself who shows up to successfully enact *our* failed Sonship.

Luke continues, and his language for Jesus is full of narrative significance:

> He has helped His servant Israel,
> In remembrance of His mercy,
> As He spoke to our fathers,
> To Abraham and to his seed forever.
> Luke 1:54-55

> To perform the mercy promised to our fathers
> And to remember His holy covenant,
> The oath which He swore to our father Abraham.
> Luke 1:72-73

> And she brought forth her firstborn Son, and wrapped Him in swaddling cloths, and laid Him in a manger, because there was no room for them in the inn. Luke 2:7

> Then the angel said to them, "Do not be afraid, for behold, I bring you good tidings of great joy which will be to all people. For there is born to

you this day in the city of David a Savior, who is
Christ the Lord." Luke 2:10-11

What's happening here is obvious now that we have the
backstory in full view. The language of birth and Sonship
is used by Luke to describe Jesus in direct relation to His
birth from the womb of the Mary, the woman, just as the
first gospel promise in Genesis 3:15 foretold. Luke is not
here setting Christ before us as God's ancient *divine* son
showing up to mingle with God's *human* sons. Rather, He
wants us to see Jesus as God Himself showing up by the
miracle of incarnation to faithfully live out the Sonship
for which all humans were made. Christ is the new man,
the representative human, the corporate Son of God in
whom all that God originally intended for humanity is
now realized. Therefore—and this is a majorly significant
point we do not want to miss—Luke intentionally traces
the genealogy of Jesus all the way back to "Adam, the
son of God" (Luke 3:38). Whereas in Matthew's Gospel
the genealogy of Jesus is given in chapter one as an
introduction to His birth, Luke places the genealogy of
Jesus after His baptism as an introduction to His public
ministry. Note the language carefully:

> When all the people were baptized, it came to pass
> that Jesus also was baptized; and while He prayed,
> the heaven was opened. And the Holy Spirit
> descended in bodily form like a dove upon Him,
> and a voice came from heaven which said, "You

are My beloved Son; in You I am well pleased."
Luke 3:21-22

You are My beloved Son.

In *You* I am well pleased.

According to Luke's telling, Jesus stands before the world as God's faithful Son in contrast to rebellious Adam. So after naming Him the "Son of God," Luke tells us of Jesus "being tempted for forty days by the devil" (Luke 4:2). Israel was tempted in the wilderness and failed. But going back earlier in the story, Adam was tempted and failed (Genesis 3). Jesus now takes on the devil and remains faithful. In Luke's telling of the gospel story, the Sonship of Jesus is like that of Adam's, placed within the narrative of Creation and the Fall, with allusions to the wilderness trials of Israel.

Adam, as God's son, was given dominion over the earth (Genesis 1:26-27). When Adam sinned, in addition to the moral aspect of the Fall, there was also a legal transfer of authority over the earth from Adam to Satan. Luke proceeds to make this clear, also, with His eye steady on Adam's story:

> Then the devil, taking Him up on a high mountain, showed Him all the kingdoms of the world in a moment of time. And the devil said to Him, "All this authority I will give You, and their glory; for this has been delivered to me, and I

give it to whomever I wish. Therefore, if You will worship before me, all will be Yours." Luke 4:5-7

Don't miss it. Luke is telling us that the devil tempted Jesus within the context of the "dominion" Adam once had over the earth as "the son of God." Satan approached Jesus by laying claim to the earth as his territory, pointing to the fact that the earth was "delivered" to him.

Delivered to him, when, by whom?

Back in Eden, by Adam!

The Fall of Adam was the point of legal transfer of earth into Satan's control. But Luke wants us to understand that in Christ we have a new Adam, a new "Son of God," who has now arrived on the scene to reverse the effects of the Fall and reclaim "dominion" over the earth.

Clearly, then, Matthew and Luke are on the same page. Both of these inspired Gospel writers identify Jesus as "the Son of God" within the narrative parameters of His earthly mission, *not* as a reference to His ancient origins. Ancient origins, ontological beginnings, metaphysical chronology—none of these interests are found anywhere in Matthew or Luke. The story they are telling is decidedly Hebrew in its concerns and completely grounded in the Old Testament.

And now, with John's Gospel, things get crazy beautiful.

"John insists that
love is the defining
characteristic of the
Sonship of Christ.
He knows the whole
point of the Messiah's
mission is to reestablish
human beings within
the social ways of
covenantal faithfulness."

CHAPTER ELEVEN
JOHN'S GOSPEL—
ONLY BEGOTTEN SON

Matthew's genealogy identifies the Sonship of Jesus with David, Abraham, and Israel.

Luke's genealogy identifies the Sonship of Jesus with Israel, as well, but also loops all the way back to Adam, thus linking the Sonship of Christ to the story of Creation.

John offers no genealogy of Christ at all, but he does define the Savior's Sonship in relation to both Adam and Israel in sync with the other Gospel writers. But he does so in his own unique way, yielding some stunning insights.

First, John takes us back to creation, identifying Jesus as none other than the Creator Himself:

> In the beginning was the Word, and the Word was with God, and the Word was God. He was in the beginning with God. All things were made through Him, and without Him nothing was made that was made. John 1:3

What a simple and profound formulation of thought. Way back "in the beginning," John explains, "God . . . was . . . with God." Not, "Son was with Father," but "God . . . was . . . with God." John is about to explain the point at which, and the sense in which, the Father-Son arrangement began. First, he takes us all the way back to "the beginning," when God embarked upon creation, and at this point in the divine reality, "God . . . was . . . with God."

So, then, reality falls into two fundamental categories, according to John: the made and the unmade. Note his language: "Without Him nothing was made that was made." Jesus, before He was Jesus, is the one who made everything, John insists, and occupied the unmade category. But then John does something astounding. He informs us that the unmade one voluntarily chose to enter the made realm by becoming part of it. The Creator became the created:

> He was in the world, and the world was made through Him, and the world did not know Him. He came to His own, and His own did not receive Him. But as many as received Him, to them He gave the right to become children of God, to those who believe in His name: who were born, not of blood, nor of the will of the flesh, nor of the will of man, but of God. And the Word became flesh and dwelt among us, and we beheld His glory, the glory as of the only begotten of the Father, full of grace and truth. John 1:10-14

Here, for the first time in the New Testament, Jesus is called, "the only begotten of the Father." If we didn't know the backstory upon which John is drawing, we might conclude that he is attempting to describe how Jesus came into existence sometime back in eternity past. But we know this is not at all what John has in mind. How do we know? Well, because John is drawing this language from the Old Testament itself, so all we have to do is go back to the Old Testament to discover exactly what it means. No guessing is necessary.

Recall what we have previously discovered. To Israel God said:

- You are my "firstborn son."

- I "begot you" when I "brought you" out of Egyptian bondage.

- In so doing, I "fathered you."

- Therefore, I am "your Father."

Continuing the father-son metaphor, God later told David, "You are My Son, *today* I have begotten You" (Psalm 2). And David says to God, "You are my Father, My God, and the rock of my salvation." And God says of David, "I will *make him* My firstborn" (Psalm 89). Once the torch of Sonship succession was passed to Solomon, God said of him, "He *shall be* My son, and *I will be* his Father" (1 Chronicles 22:10). In each instance—with Solomon, David, and Israel—they are made God's sons, not by biological birth, but by calling to the covenant vocation. In the biblical story, Israel was God's only begotten son among all the nations of the earth, whose job it was to so powerfully witness to God's glory that many other nations would become God's sons as well. Once we understand this narrative dynamic, we understand the whole point of the Bible, and we understand the sense in which Jesus is God's only begotten Son. This brings us back to our passage in the first chapter of John.

When John calls Jesus "the only begotten of the Father," he is identifying Him as the one in whom Israel's calling will be finally and fully actualized. Whereas Israel failed in its witness to the nations and, therefore, failed to draw the nations into their own Sonship relationship with God, Jesus will succeed. He became the Son of God so that we might become the same—that we might be given the "right to become children of God." The one who made the world took on the Sonship role so that we might be incorporated back into that role ourselves.

That's the point of John's Gospel. He is not exploring Greek questions about God's metaphysical origin, but Hebrew questions regarding the narrative calling of Israel coming to fulfillment in the Messiah. But if we have any doubt that John, like the other Gospel writers, has the Old Testament narrative in view as he introduces Jesus as God's "only begotten son," we can banish that doubt when we come to the end of John 1:

> Nathanael answered and said to Him, "Rabbi, You are the Son of God! You are the King of Israel!"
> John 1:49

In John's telling of the story, Jesus is "the Son of God" in the sense that He is "the King of Israel." These are equivalent identities. The Sonship of Christ designates His covenantal identity in the lineage of David, not His ontological origin in some ancient lineage of divine beings who engage in some mysterious begetting process, one god giving birth to another, as if we're dealing with Greek mythology.

Then we come to John 3:16, which is the most familiar biblical passage regarding the Sonship of Christ, and the main verse upon which the anti-Trinitarian doctrine rests:

> For God so loved the world that He gave His only begotten Son, that whoever believes in Him should not perish but have everlasting life.

The verse has a context, both an immediate context and a larger narrative context. In John 3, Jesus has a conversation with a Pharisee by the name of Nicodemus. Right away, He dives into His mission as "the Son of God" and "the King of Israel," leaving no room for misunderstanding:

> Most assuredly, I say to you, unless one is born again, he cannot see the kingdom of God.
> John 3:3

Nicodemus, if he is to "see the kingdom of God," must be "born again."

What?

Why is Jesus talking about rebirth?

And what does the kingdom of God have to do with it?

Well, if we track with the story John is telling, something utterly brilliant and breathtaking will emerge to our understanding. "The King of Israel" has now come, John explains, to establish His "kingdom." Which is to say, "the Son of God" has now come to restore Sonship status to humanity. So in order to get in on the new kingdom, we need to be "born again."

Born again?

What does that mean?

The idea of new birth makes sense for John because the entire Old Testament is built around birth—the birth of the firstborn son for the fulfillment of the covenant promise. Jesus has now come into our world to fulfill Israel's vocation as God's firstborn son, and He is inviting all other human beings to be reborn as sons of God as well. To be born again means, therefore, to enter into the new Genesis Jesus is launching as the new Son of God who has now come to replace Adam and reenact Israel's covenant history with faithfulness.

To what end?

To the end that the kingdom of God would be established and eventually fill the whole earth, as God promised to Abraham: "In you all the families of the earth shall be blessed" (Genesis 12:3). Jesus, when He arrives as the "Son of God" and "the King of Israel" to establish the kingdom of God on earth, invites Nicodemus, and all of us, to be "born again" into this new arrangement of the world. In other words, He invites us to become covenant sons of God through which God's covenant ways can overtake the world.

It is in this context that Jesus identifies Himself as God's "only begotten Son." Surely this language means that the Father, way back in eternity past, gave birth to Jesus, before which Jesus did not have existence distinct from God?

Actually, it means nothing of the sort. Such concerns are nowhere on John's radar.

We can only interpret John's Sonship language as possessing metaphysical concerns if we ignore the big story Scripture is telling us. But the moment we begin to think within the trajectory of Adam, Abraham, Isaac, Jacob, Israel, and David, a totally different picture comes into focus. The New Testament comes alive with narrative significance, and John 3:16 itself finally opens like a flower to our understanding.

Let's dig deeper by simply asking the question, is Jesus the *only* "only begotten son" in Scripture? We already know the answer, don't we?

> By faith Abraham, when he was tested, offered up Isaac, and he who had received the promises offered up his only begotten son. Hebrews 11:17

There you have it!

Isaac bears the title "only begotten son," just as Israel as a nation and David as Israel's king would later bear the same title. "Only begotten son" is a covenant title, not a chronological or ontological title. If we don't know the story of Scripture, we will tend to be confused by Isaac being called Abraham's "only begotten son." After all, the Bible plainly tells us that Abraham had, not one, but eight sons: Ishmael, Isaac, Jokshan, Zimran, Midian, Ishbak, Shuah, and Medan (Genesis 25:1-9). So how can Isaac be called Abraham's "only begotten son"? It's very simple, once you see it. Isaac was *not* Abraham's only begotten biological son, nor was he even Abraham's firstborn son chronologically. Isaac was Abraham's only begotten *covenant* son. And that is precisely what Jesus means when He calls Himself God's "only begotten Son." By appropriating the title to Himself, Jesus is explaining to Nicodemus that He is the messianic antitype of Isaac, and Israel, and David, and Solomon.

So, then, John 3:16 is not a declaration that Jesus was literally "begotten" of God way back before coming to our world, nor that Jesus came into distinct existence chronologically after God. Rather, John 3:16 is telling us that Jesus is the fulfillment of the covenant promise foreshadowed in Israel's covenantal Sonship. The end goal of the biblical story is that God would have a faithful son, a son who would keep covenant with God and with humanity, a son who would become the source of many other faithful sons, reproducing the image of God within the wider human race. Jesus is God's Son in this sense. He is Adam as God meant Adam to be, Israel as God meant Israel to be, David as God meant David to be, humanity as God meant humanity to be.

Now we can read John 3:16 for what it actually means within the narrative flow of Scripture.

GOD
the covenant-keeping God of Israel

so loved
with the unfailing faithfulness of His covenant oath

the world
the entire Hebrew and Gentile population of earth that God told Abraham He would bless through his offspring

that He gave His only begotten Son
just as He promised He would, through all the prophets, as foreshadowed in Isaac, Abraham's "only begotten son" of promise, and as typified in David, God's messianic Son of the eternal covenant kingdom

that whosoever
Jews and Gentiles alike

believes in Him
as Abraham believed the covenant promise of God

should not perish
under the covenant curses stipulated by Moses

but have everlasting life
as promised in the covenant blessings stipulated by Moses

Or, stated more succinctly:

God so loved, with covenant faithfulness, the whole world,
both Jews and Gentiles, that He gave to the whole world
His only begotten Son of promise to demonstrate what
true Sonship looks like, so that whoever believes in Him as
God's faithful Son and is born again through Him into true
Sonship, should not perish under the covenant curses, but
have everlasting life under the covenant blessings.

It is unlikely that you have ever read John 3:16 like this,
because this most famous of all biblical passages has been
so dislodged from its narrative context that almost nobody
hears what it's actually saying. As a result, the term "only
begotten Son" is open to gross misinterpretation, as if Jesus
was trying to tell us how He came to exist distinct from the
Father in some ancient, ethereal past. But once we take in
the entire scope of the story, it becomes clear that John 3:16
is not about the ontological origins of Jesus, but about His
covenant identity as the Son of God and His good news of
our reinduction into the Sonship covenant through Him.

In the first of his letters, John also delves into the logic of
the biblical story by drawing a clear line of connection

between Christ's status as God's "only begotten Son"
and the call for human beings to be reborn into the
same status:

> Beloved, let us love one another, for love is of
> God; and everyone who loves is born of God and
> knows God. He who does not love does not know
> God, for God is love. In this the love of God was
> manifested toward us, that God has sent His only
> begotten Son into the world, that we might live
> through Him. In this is love, not that we loved
> God, but that He loved us and sent His Son to
> be the propitiation for our sins. Beloved, if God
> so loved us, we also ought to love one another.
> 1 John 4:7-11

John insists that "love" is the defining characteristic of
the Sonship of Christ. He knows the whole point of the
Messiah's mission is to reestablish human beings within
the social ways of covenantal faithfulness. Jesus is God's
"only begotten Son" precisely because He is the one in
whom God's love is finally and fully realized within the
human realm. Clearly, John is framing the work of Christ
within the covenant narrative of the Old Testament. He is,
therefore, using the title "only begotten Son" in the same
way the prophets before him used it—to signal the arrival
of the faithful covenant Son of God.

John knows God made a covenant with Abraham. He
also knows the prophets defined that covenant as God's

"unfailing love" and that they foretold the coming of a Son through whom the covenant of love would be fulfilled (Isaiah 54:10; 42:6, NIV). So when John looks upon Jesus, he sees Him launching a new humanity characterized by the very love foretold by all the prophets. So in that context, John can press his point home: "everyone who loves is born of God." The "only begotten Son" position of Christ is the starting point from which a new kind of humanity can be born. In Christ, God has now come to make good on His promise to bless *all* humans through *one* human, to bless *all* the nations of the earth through *one* nation. Israel's purpose will now be realized in Jesus. The world will be redeemed through the deeds of God's one and only faithful Son. And each of us is invited to be "born again" into the Sonship identity He has now reclaimed for us.

The point is, John 3:16 means what it means and doesn't mean what it doesn't mean. And we are not justified in imposing on the text what we think it means. Yes, Jesus is God's "only begotten son," but John's Gospel gives no indication that this means He was begotten *as God from God* sometime in the ancient past. According to John's immediate context and the larger biblical context as a whole, "Son of God" is a human identity, not a divine one. The very God who made the world, in John's telling, has become flesh and perfected the Sonship role as our new covenant-keeping head, as Adam's replacement and Israel's Messiah. Every human being may now find access to the same identity through union with Him.

The message of Jesus is simply and profoundly this: *I am God's only begotten Son, and I'm inviting you to be born again so you might share the position of faithful Sonship with Me.*

So amazing!

Now, if you think John's framing of the Sonship of Christ is eye-opening, you're going to get at least equally excited about what Paul has to say in Romans.

"The truth of the Bible belongs only to those who read the whole book. Everyone else is destined for confusion and theological weirdness."

CHAPTER TWELVE

ROMANS—GOD'S FIRSTBORN SON

The Sonship of Christ figures prominently into Paul's thinking in the book of Romans. His line of reasoning is simple and powerful: God Himself became the Son of God in order to reestablish humanity in its rightful Sonship position.

Right out of the gate, as Paul introduces the gospel, he writes with a full awareness that Jesus is the Son of God within the lineage of Israel and King David:

> Paul, a bondservant of Jesus Christ, called to be an apostle, separated to the gospel of God which He promised before through His prophets in the Holy Scriptures, concerning His Son Jesus Christ our Lord, who was born of the seed of David according to the flesh, and declared to be the Son of God with power according to the Spirit of holiness, by the resurrection from the dead.
> Romans 1:1-4

Do not fail to notice that Jesus was "*declared* to be," or "*appointed*" to be (NIV), "the Son of God" by virtue of His "resurrection from the dead." Sonship is not His innate, eternal identity, but rather a role He took up for a purpose. This is emphasized by the fact that Paul says Jesus was "declared to be the Son of God" by virtue of two realities: (1) because He was born in the lineage of David and (2) because He was victorious over death due to His alignment with "the Spirit of holiness." In other words, His character lined up with His lineage, which could not be said of David, nor of Israel, nor of Adam. This unequivocally demonstrates that the New Testament is not addressing the ancient ontology of Christ when calling Him God's Son, but rather His covenant identity in David's genealogical lineage.

As we've already seen, both Luke and John understood Jesus to be God's Son in the sense that Adam was God's son. Paul does the same in Romans 5, where he plainly states that Adam was "a type of Him who was to come," speaking of Jesus (verse 14). Paul then explains further:

> For if by the one man's offense many died, much more the grace of God and the gift by the grace of the one Man, Jesus Christ, abounded to many. And the gift is not like that which came through the one who sinned. For the judgment which came from one offense resulted in condemnation, but the free gift which came from many offenses resulted in justification. For if by the one man's offense death reigned through the one, much more those who receive abundance of grace and of the gift of righteousness will reign in life through the One, Jesus Christ. Therefore, as through one man's offense judgment came to all men, resulting in condemnation, even so through one Man's righteous act the free gift came to all men, resulting in justification of life. For as by one man's disobedience many were made sinners, so also by one Man's obedience many will be made righteous. Romans 5:15-19

According to Paul, we have two representative heads before us, or two archetypal human beings: Adam and Christ.

Adam was the original man, created in the image of God, and endowed with the capacity to procreate in his own image. But Adam sinned and thereby brought death upon the entire human race.

Christ has now come as the new man, the second Adam, through whom the first Adam's failure is rectified, so that "through one Man's righteous act the free gift came to all men," and "by one Man's obedience many will be made righteous." Christ is the one Man that now represents all men in the sense that in Him we now have a new beginning from which to start, free from sin and guilt.

Having reminded us of the old man, Adam, and introduced to us the new man, Jesus, Paul then invites us to identify with the new man through the symbolic act of baptism:

> Or do you not know that as many of us as were baptized into Christ Jesus were baptized into His death? Therefore we were buried with Him through baptism into death, that just as Christ was raised from the dead by the glory of the Father, even so we also should walk in newness of life. Romans 6:3-4

The Christ event—His life, death, burial, and resurrection—was enacted for us, in our stead, to the end that we would be reincorporated into the Sonship position Jesus forged out for us. When we are baptized, we are essentially saying we have disavowed our first birth in the lineage of the first Adam and relocated our identity in the second Adam, Jesus Christ. You will recall that this is precisely what Jesus taught in John 3: "You must be born again." In other words, you must be reestablished in your Sonship position by breaking ranks with Adam and taking up your new identity in Christ.

In Romans 8, Paul further works out the implications of the Sonship of Christ:

> For as many as are led by the Spirit of God, these are sons of God. For you did not receive the spirit of bondage again to fear, but you received the Spirit of adoption by whom we cry out, "Abba, Father." The Spirit Himself bears witness with our spirit that we are children of God, and if children, then heirs—heirs of God and joint heirs with Christ, if indeed we suffer with Him, that we may also be glorified together. Romans 8:14-17

In Paul's understanding, we become "sons of God" through the Sonship of Christ. Through Jesus, we undergo an "adoption" process and, in this way, we are made members of God's family. We "cry out" with a completely new sense of identity, "Abba, Father." When we become "children of God," Paul explains, we become "joint heirs with Christ." We inherit all that He, by His faithful

Sonship, has inherited. And what is that? Well, basically the whole world, just as God had promised the whole world to Abraham and his posterity (Genesis 12; Daniel 7:27; Hebrews 1:2; Revelation 21:7). With this powerful framing of the gospel, Paul has brought us full circle back to Genesis, to the stewardship vocation of humanity. The grand goal of the adoption process is that the earth would be brought back under human rule:

> For the earnest expectation of the creation eagerly waits for the revealing of the sons of God. For the creation was subjected to futility, not willingly, but because of Him who subjected it in hope; because the creation itself also will be delivered from the bondage of corruption into the glorious liberty of the children of God. Romans 8:19-21

Why is creation itself longing for the reinstating of human beings to their position as sons of God? Because, quite simply, human beings, created in the image of God, were set over creation to live out the covenant of love as faithful stewards of the planet. When we become who we are meant to be, Paul explains, "the creation itself also will be delivered from the bondage of corruption into the glorious liberty of the children of God." So, then, Jesus is the Son of God, as Adam was, for the purpose of procreating many other sons of God in His image:

> For whom He foreknew, He also predestined to be conformed to the image of His Son, that He

might be the firstborn among many brethren.
Romans 8:29

Again, Paul has looped all the way back to the Genesis
account of Creation. God created Adam and Eve in God's
"own image" (Genesis 1:27). Then Adam "begot a son in his
own likeness, after his image" (Genesis 5:3). According to
Paul, Jesus is Adam's replacement. He is, therefore, the new
progenitor of the human race, whose job it is to reproduce
many other sons in the image of God. Jesus is God's
"firstborn" Son "among many brethren," Paul explains.
That is, He inaugurated a new Sonship lineage, within
which many others will be reborn as His spiritual progeny.
Jesus is the "firstborn" Son of God, not *chronologically*, but
covenantally. Clearly, then, Paul is most emphatically not
telling us anything about the pre-incarnate origins of Jesus.
That concern is nowhere on his radar.

Several times the New Testament calls Jesus God's
"firstborn" Son (Romans 8:29; Colossians 1:15, 18;
Hebrews 1:6; Revelation 1:5). Many have been befuddled
by this way of describing Jesus. By contrast, other New
Testament passages state that Jesus is God manifested
in the flesh. Why, then, is He described as God's
firstborn Son?

Well, our befuddlement is deserved.

Our evangelistic scholarship has generally handled the
Bible as a prooftext manual from which to construct

propositional arguments. As a result, we have often failed to take in the grand narrative arc of Scripture. Therefore we have struggled to make sense of this New Testament way of describing Jesus, and the New Testament in general. Failing to see that the Sonship terminology of the New Testament has its intended meaning within the unfolding story of the Old Testament, we don't know what to make of Jesus . . . um . . . God, being described as God's "firstborn Son." So we come up with various strained and elaborate metaphysical explanations that are nowhere found in the Bible:

"Well, you see, yeah, of course, He's God, but a long time ago He was, you know, born. But He was the firstborn Son of God, so that makes Him different, you know. Because He is the first one God ever birthed, He's God, so that birthing process must have been, you know, unique, making Him God, even though really there's only one God. Yeah, you know, it's a mystery, but it must have happened because the Bible says it happened."

Actually, no, the Bible says none of that or anything like it.

Our problem is, we see verses and words when we ought to see the story that gives the verses and words their meaning.

We see isolated lines of information when we ought to see characters and themes moving toward a cohesive endgoal.

We see detached pieces of data from which we construct theological arguments when we ought to see a big and beautiful story that interprets itself without us making stuff up and imposing it on the story.

The truth of the Bible belongs *only* to those who read the whole book. Everyone else is destined for confusion and theological weirdness. Those who merely parse words and compile verses will inevitably miss the point of Scripture and formulate false doctrines that are out of sync with its grand plot line.

Taking the whole story into account, we easily discover why and in what sense Jesus is called God's "firstborn Son." The title has a specific intent that only makes sense within the Old Testament context. Early in the biblical narrative, as we have already noted, God vows to save the human race from the inside, by means of a daring and compassionate act of solidarity. A child will be born to the human race who will undo the Fall (Genesis 3:15). The promise echoes down through the generations, and around that promise a sense of anticipation develops with all eyes fixed on the womb of womankind. Within this narrative there are three key Old Testament passages that employ the word "firstborn," each one grounded in the time they were written and each one pointing forward to Christ:

Israel is My son, My firstborn. Exodus 4:22

> I am a Father to Israel, and Ephraim is My
> firstborn. Jeremiah 31:9

> He shall cry to Me, "You are my Father, My God,
> and the rock of my salvation." Also I will make
> him My firstborn, the highest of the kings of
> the earth. My mercy I will keep for him forever,
> and My covenant shall stand firm with him.
> Psalm 89:26-28

Each of these passages employ the concept of "firstborn"
in a covenantal sense, not in a chronological sense. The
first two depict God relating to Israel as His firstborn son.
The third refers to King David as God's firstborn son.
Neither Israel nor David was God's firstborn son in the
flow of chronological time. The point is not chronology,
but position and calling. Now, Romans 8:29 makes sense:

> For whom He foreknew, He also predestined to be
> conformed to the image of His Son, that He might
> be the firstborn among many brethren.

Following the narrative arc of Romans, Paul here conflates
the story of Adam and the story of Israel, indicating that
both were prototypical of Christ. God's goal, Paul says,
is that human beings would be, as originally intended,
"conformed" to His "image." Adam failed to reflect God's
image as God's "firstborn" son. Israel was then called
to bear the image of God as His "firstborn" son. But
Israel also failed. Jesus has now come, Paul says, to fulfill

the Sonship ideal. Therefore He is God's new and true "firstborn" Son. He is the one in whom Adam's failure and Israel's failure are reversed. Jesus reconstituted the "image" of God in humanity. As a result of His faithful Sonship, He will be "the firstborn among many brethren." That is, many more children of God will arise from Him since He is the new head of the human race. And these "many" more, according to Hebrews 12:23, constitute "the general assembly and church of the firstborn who are registered in heaven." Adam failed to retain the "image" of God, so God Himself became incarnate in order to demonstrate what it looks like to really be human as we were meant to be, bearing God's image, or loving like God loves with covenantal faithfulness. Thus Jesus "is the image of the invisible God, the firstborn over all creation" (Colossians 1:15). Creation has a new starting point in Christ.

Jesus is also twice called "the firstborn from the dead," once by Paul and once by John, both times referring to His resurrection (Colossians 1:18; Revelation 1:5). He is the firstborn from the dead in that His resurrection makes the resurrection of countless others possible. Even here, "first" does not suggest first in time. With regard to chronology, Jesus was *not* the first person ever raised from the dead. We know from Scripture that at least two individuals were resurrected before Jesus: Moses and Lazarus (Matthew 17:3; Jude 1:9; John 11). Jesus is not the firstborn from the dead *chronologically*, but rather *positionally*. His resurrection is *the* victory over death that makes all other resurrections possible.

So, then, when the New Testament writers call Jesus God's "firstborn," they have no concern whatsoever with His metaphysical origins or the chronology of His existence in relation to the Father. He is not God's "firstborn" because He was literally the first being God gave birth to way back sometime before the creation of our world. Rather, He was designated as the firstborn Son of God directly parallel to Israel's national identity as God's firstborn son. Having come to our world by means of incarnation, Jesus became the corporate embodiment of Israel, and all of humanity. The only time Jesus was ever "born" was at the point of His incarnation via the womb of Mary. Before that, He was nothing less than eternal God, having no point of beginning. To say otherwise is to break ranks with the biblical narrative and to do so without any biblical support. As we've systematically noted so far in this study, one-by-one, every New Testament usage of the title "Son of God" with reference to Jesus is directly and deliberately derived from the Old Testament script.

We've covered a lot of ground in this chapter, so let's conclude by making sure we are tracking with Paul's reasoning in Romans:

- Jesus is the Son of David. As the Son of David, He is the Son of God. They are one and the same role (Romans 1).

- As the Son of God, Jesus is, in the larger narrative, our new Adam, through whom sin and death are negated and we have access to a whole new human potential (Romans 5).

- As our new Adam, Jesus lived, died, and rose from the dead to establish for us a new human identity, with which we identify through baptism (Romans 6).

- As the Son of God in the Davidic and Adamic sense, Jesus has lifted condemnation from us so that we can be adopted as sons of God, regain God's image, and become joint heirs with Him of the very world we lost through Adam. Occupying the position vacated by Adam, and then by Israel, Jesus is God's new and true firstborn human Son, from whom many more sons will emerge (Romans 8).

What a breathtaking vision of Christ and His achievements on our behalf!

But all of this meaningful and beautiful gospel theology is lost if we push the Sonship of Christ off into some unique identity that He alone possesses from eternity past. None of Paul's narrative logic makes any sense if we work from the premise that Jesus is God's Son in an ancient, ontological sense. Paul's whole point is that Jesus is the Son of God in the sense that Adam was, within the framework of the covenant narrative of the Old Testament, so that His Sonship is our new beginning. We, through His Sonship, regain our position as sons of God.

"In the most
monumental and
paradoxical act of
empathetic love
imaginable, God
became the Son of
God and is now our
eternal Brother."

CHAPTER THIRTEEN

HEBREWS—OUR ETERNAL BROTHER

In the book of Hebrews, the Sonship of Christ is clearly depicted as a covenant role that began to be executed at His birth. This is not merely a theological point to be proven, it is a vital truth freighted with experiential riches beyond estimation. To miss it is to miss the deeply personal point of the entire salvation enterprise.

So let's think this through very carefully.

> God, who at various times and in various
> ways spoke in time past to the fathers by the
> prophets, has in these last days spoken to us
> by His Son, whom He has appointed heir of all
> things, through whom also He made the worlds;
> who being the brightness of His glory and the
> express image of His person, and upholding all
> things by the word of His power, when He had
> by Himself purged our sins, sat down at the right
> hand of the Majesty on high, having become
> so much better than the angels, as He has by
> inheritance obtained a more excellent name than
> they. Hebrews 1:1-4

This is big stuff to ponder.

First, the author of Hebrews announces that Jesus, as God's "last days . . . Son," after "He had by Himself purged our sins, sat down at the right hand of the Majesty on high." As a result, He has "become so much better than the angels, as He has by inheritance obtained a more excellent name than they."

If the author of Hebrews wants us to operate on the assumption that Jesus is God's eternal, ontological Son prior to His incarnation, there would be no sense in speaking of Jesus *becoming* better than the angels and *obtaining* a more excellent name than they. If His Sonship refers to His eternal nature, He could never be thought of as having been *less* than the angels. Clearly, the point here is that Jesus, as the human Son of God in the Adamic sense, *by means of the incarnation*, has achieved things *as a human being* that has elevated Him, and humanity as a whole with Him, to a position that is above the angels. This becomes even clearer as the author's line of reasoning continues.

In Hebrew 1:5, the Father addresses Jesus as, "My Son," by virtue of the fact that "*today* I have begotten You."

There's that word "begotten" again, which we encountered in John 3:16. Notice that Hebrews is about to tell us *when* this begetting took place. God says to Jesus, "You are My Son, *today* I have begotten You."

Today?

Meaning, *when*, exactly?

The answer is explicit in the passage: "when He brings the firstborn into the world" (verse 6).

Jesus became God's "begotten" and "firstborn" Son at the point of His birth to our world. So the Father says, "I *will be* to Him a Father, and He *shall be* to Me a Son," not, "*I am* to Him a Father and *He is* to Me a Son." They were *now* entering into these roles toward one another.

They, who?

The author of Hebrews goes on to tell us who they were to one another before becoming Father and Son to one another:

> Your throne, O God, is forever and ever; a
> scepter of righteousness is the scepter of Your
> kingdom. You have loved righteousness and
> hated lawlessness; therefore God, Your God, has
> anointed You with the oil of gladness more than
> Your companions . . . You, Lord, in the beginning
> laid the foundation of the earth, and the heavens
> are the work of Your hands. Hebrews 1:8-10

Astounding!

Leaving no confusion as to Christ's innate identity, the Father addresses the Son as "God" and calls Him "Lord." And then the Father says to Him, I am "Your God." Each one is God to the other, because, in fact, each one is God.

And one of these persons that was always and only God in eternity past, became the "Son of God" in order to model Sonship to our world of fallen sons.

For the author of Hebrews, Jesus is the new corporate, representative head of the human family. And from this strategic position—as a full-fledged member of the human race—He will reverse the effects of the Fall and elevate the human race to the position originally intended for it. So with this end in view, the author of Hebrews goes on to tell us that "the world to come" will not be "in subjection to angels" (Hebrews 2:5), but rather to Christ and His human brethren. God became human (the incarnation), and then took humanity with Him (in His resurrection and ascension) to the throne of the universe. Human beings were made, we are then told, "for a little while lower than the angels" (verse 7, ESV).

Now there's a theological idea of massive proportions!

"For *a little while* lower than the angels"?

This language indicates a temporary or provisional status that is to be surpassed. The Fall of Adam and Eve interrupted God's original plan for human development. If our original representative heads (Genesis 1:28) had remained in faithful relation to God and one another, the human race, as God's unique image-bearers, would have naturally superseded the angelic order in some sense, perhaps in intimacy with God and in general servant-leadership of the entire universe. All that was forfeited by the Fall.

But wait, there is good news!

Hebrews is telling us that God has achieved something of cosmic significance in Christ. He has become the agent through which the original plan will go forward. Due to God's unfailing love, the plan will go forward through Christ.

> For in that He (God) put all in subjection under him (mankind), He (God) left nothing that is not put under him (mankind). But now we do not yet see all things put under him (humankind). But we see Jesus, who was made a little lower than the angels (by means of His incarnation), for the suffering of death crowned with glory and honor, that He, by the grace of God, might taste death for everyone. For it was fitting for Him, for whom are all things and by whom are all things, in bringing many sons to glory, to make the captain of their salvation perfect through sufferings. For both He who sanctifies (Jesus) and those who are being sanctified (human beings) are all of one (humanity), for which reason He is not ashamed to call them brethren (fellow sons of God), saying: "I will declare Your name to My brethren; in the midst of the assembly I will sing praise to You." And again: "I will put My trust in Him." And again:

"Here am I and the children whom God has given Me." Hebrews 2:8-13

This is a dense and rich passage. Let's break it down into bite size pieces:

- Looping back to verse 7, we are told that God's original intent was that humanity would occupy the highest position in creation, even above the angels.

- That plan was thwarted by the fall of the human race, so we do not now see human beings occupying their rightful position.

- But we do see Jesus, as the Son of God, occupying the rightful position of humanity.

- Taking on human nature, Jesus tasted death for everyone and was then exalted to the right hand of God, still bearing human nature and thus holding His Sonship status.

- He did this so He could bring "many sons to glory"— in other words, reestablish human beings in the Sonship position they were meant to occupy all along.

- Jesus became a true and proper human son to God as Adam should have been, thus redeeming Adam's failure and modeling Sonship for the human race, thereby bringing us into a restored position of true

Sonship. Therefore, "He is not ashamed to call them brethren."

- Having become one of us, Christ executed the task of declaring God's name to humanity, thus eliciting our praise to God in the light of His good character.

- As a human being, Jesus put His trust in God as Adam should have done, thus opening the way for the restoration of our trust in God.

- Having achieved all of this, Jesus presents Himself to God along with "the children" He won back to God.

The book of Hebrews, like Romans and like the Gospels, clearly renders the Sonship of Christ as the climactic unfolding of the Old Testament narrative. All of His activity as God's Son occurs within the human realm, beginning at the point of His incarnation. Adam was the son of God by creation. Christ became the Son of God by incarnation.

It is precisely because Jesus is the offspring of the woman that He is the Son of God. The incarnation was the act by which He became the Son of God. He came to our world to live out, in our very flesh, a life of covenantal trust toward God—to live *as* us and to model *for* us what true Sonship looks like. In the most monumental and paradoxical act of empathetic love imaginable, God became the Son of God and is now our eternal Brother, from which flows the cataclysmic punch line:

A fully realized Son of God sits upon the throne of the universe awaiting our arrival, eager that we reign with Him.

Because He is now eternally one with us, we are eternally one with Him. Human nature has been grafted into the divine nature. Whatever position Christ now occupies, He occupies as a member of the human race and as our new representative head. Therefore, we are invited to occupy that position with Him. He is there *for* us, literally *as* us. What He inherits, we inherit with Him (Hebrews 1:2; Revelation 21:7; Romans 8:16-17). What He rules, we rule with Him (Daniel 7:27; Revelation 3:21).

All of this is, of course, utterly astounding. No God-story more intensely personal, nor more profoundly true to our deepest intuitions of identity, has ever been told.

The entire thought process of Hebrews 1 and 2 is built on the premise that the Sonship of Christ is a solidarity position He has taken up with humanity. The moment we redefine the Sonship of Christ as His unique, divine, ontological identity, none of what we've just discovered about human destiny in Christ can be logically deduced. He became what, by nature, He was not—namely, the Son of God—so that we might become what we, by nature, were always meant to be—namely, sons and daughters of God. And this brings us to the perfect position for exploring the title Jesus favors most for Himself:

The Son of Man.

"By His covenant-
confirming death on
the cross, Jesus has
conquered the usurping
ruler of this world and
returned the earth to
human lordship."

CHAPTER FOURTEEN
SON OF MAN

The prophetic book of Daniel presents a vital piece of the Bible's Sonship narrative. In fact, much of the New Testament makes no sense unless Daniel's visions are taken into account.

The key figure in Daniel bears the title, "the Son of Man," which was the title Jesus used for Himself more than any other—more than 90 times in the four Gospels. By repeatedly calling Himself "the Son of Man"—all the while living out the principles of the new kingdom He came to establish—Jesus was specifically identifying Himself as the cryptic personage who, in Daniel's visions, overturns all the power structures of our world and establishes a completely new arrangement of the world.

If we fail to read the New Testament against the backdrop Daniel erects for us, we will inevitably reduce the gospel to a self-centered concern for personal salvation and a postmortem heavenly home. Daniel, by contrast, drills down into the way things operate in this present world. He delves into the way things *are* versus the way things *ought to be* and finally *will be*. Amid all the egocentric power-mongering that characterizes the empires of our fallen world, Daniel foretells the coming of a kingdom that rules by the counter-intuitive ways of humility and self-sacrifice. In keeping with the entire biblical narrative, Daniel informs us that God will establish His radically different kingdom as an inside job, from within humanity's own genetic realm. The alternative order of things, in other words, will be established by "the Son of Man."

Before jumping directly into Daniel's revelation of "the Son of Man," let's consider the back story leading up to the book of Daniel, because, as we've realized repeatedly in our journey, the truer truth of Scripture belongs exclusively to those who grasp its grand narrative.

God created Adam and Eve and gave them "dominion over the earth" (Genesis 1:26). This is delegation language. The first humans were given the power of self-governance. "The heaven, even the heavens, are the Lord's; but the earth He has given to the children of men" (Psalm 115:16). They were to rule the world according to their God-given identity as bearers of the divine image. "God is love" (1 John 4:16). Adam and Eve were to live in freely chosen harmony with God, with one another, and with the earth. Their rulership over the world was to be of a particular quality. They were to govern from the relational premise of other-centeredness, procreating the image of God from generation to generation, thus perpetuating a benevolent lordship of the world.

The fall of mankind was, therefore, more than a moral fall. It was also a governmental fall. Grab hold of this idea, because it becomes vitally significant as we delve into Daniel. By violating the relational integrity of love between themselves and God, and between one another, Adam and Eve essentially set in motion a different

134 THE SONSHIP OF CHRIST

governing principle, a different way of relating, and in so doing they abdicated their position of rulership over the world. Now the earth, along with its human inhabitants, was under the control of a foreign lord, Satan himself. This is why the Bible ascribes to the fallen angel titles of dominion over the world. He is called,

> . . . the ruler of this world. John 12:31; 14:30; 16:11

> . . . the god of this age. 2 Corinthians 4:4

> . . . the prince of the power of the air, the spirit who now works in the sons of disobedience. Ephesians 2:2

By telling us Satan is "the prince of the power of the air," Paul is not speaking literally, as if Satan were in charge of the oxygen supply. Rather, Satan is the unseen spiritual force that feeds the selfish impulses of humanity for the formation of the cultural, social, economic, political, and ideological systems. As the ruler of this world, Satan is the instigating mind behind the governing principles upon which the kingdoms of this world operate. "We know," John matter-of-factly informs us, "that we are of God, and the whole world lies under the sway of the wicked one" (1 John 5:19). The world is under the influence of a dark ruler who prompts humanity to establish systems of governance in his image. Once the principle of selfishness was introduced into human makeup, all relationships began to disintegrate.

Adam aligned himself against Eve in an effort to preserve himself (Genesis 3).

Cain murdered his brother Abel in the first recorded act of human violence (Genesis 4).

Violence became the norm, people seeking to control and dominate one another to the point that the human race was brought to the brink of extinction, making it necessary for God to intervene with a flood and start over with Noah and his family (Genesis 6-9).

After the Flood, human beings began to consolidate their power and to cultivate the inclination toward self-exaltation and force, giving rise to Nimrod, the mighty man, from whom arose the world's first empire. Babylon became the iconic domination system in the biblical story, setting the stage for monarchy (one man ruling over many) as the natural governing system of fallen mankind (Genesis 10-11).

God called Abram and Sarai out of Babylon to initiate a different kind of social structure based on the relational dynamic of covenant, or self-giving love, promising to give them a son, who would have a son, who would have a son, and so on until a son would finally be born through whom all the families of the earth would be blessed (Genesis 12-38).

As the story continues, the covenant lineage is established with Abraham, Isaac, Jacob, and Jacob's twelve sons, but not without the necessity of God navigating their relational dysfunction (Genesis 39-50).

As the story unfolds, Israel is taken into bondage under the despotic rule of Egypt, a kingdom defined by monarchy (one man ruling over many) and materialistic exploitation of human beings (Exodus 1-2).

Israel is eventually delivered from Egyptian bondage, not by a king with a military, but by a prophet with a message (Exodus 3).

Once they are free, Moses tells the people of Israel that God will establish them as His covenant nation and that God will lead them by the establishment of a system of laws (Exodus 2:24; 6:4-5; 19:5), a system of laws that will be based on the single relational dynamic of love (Leviticus 19:18; Deuteronomy 6:5).

As a prophet, not a king, Moses organizes Israel under the world's first constitutional legal system, moving toward the equality of all persons before the law, without "partiality," which was an unheard-of system in a world that only knew the despotic rule of kings. "I will do marvels such as have not been done in all the earth, nor in any nation," God explains the covenant system, "and all the people among whom you are shall see the work of the Lord. For it is an awesome thing that I will do with you" (Exodus 34:10; Deuteronomy 1:4-5, 16-17).

Marvelous and awesome, for sure!

With Israel, God was essentially seeking to establish a non-monarchical community of covenantal love, in which human beings could grow into their potential for self-governance. In a world defined by intellectual ignorance, moral degradation, generational abuse, hierarchical dictatorship, self-serving social chaos, and theological darkness, God selected a people group, separated them from the world's imploding systems, and established a social structure based on the impartial rule of law, grounded in the principle of love. The goal was that Israel would operate as a "kingdom of priests" in order to mediate the knowledge of God's ways to the surrounding nations and attract them into the covenant system of living (Exodus 19:5).

The witness was to be powerful. If obeyed, the covenant of love would elevate Israel in every way and on all levels—physically, spiritually, morally, agriculturally, economically, politically, and relationally. Moses explained the stunning plan:

> See, I have taught you decrees and laws as the Lord my God commanded me, so that you may follow them in the land you are entering to take possession of it. Observe them carefully, for this will show your

wisdom and understanding to the nations, who
will hear about all these decrees and say, 'Surely this
great nation is a wise and understanding people.'
What other nation is so great as to have their gods
near them the way the Lord our God is near us
whenever we pray to him? And what other nation
is so great as to have such righteous decrees and
laws as this body of laws I am setting before you
today? . . . Keep his decrees and commands, which I
am giving you today, so that it may go well with you
and your children after you and that you may live
long in the land the Lord your God gives you for all
time. Deuteronomy 4:5-8, 40, NIV

Oh, that their hearts would be inclined to fear
me and keep all my commands always, so that
it might go well with them and their children
forever! Deuteronomy 5:29, NIV

Now it shall come to pass, if you diligently obey the
voice of the Lord your God, to observe carefully
all His commandments which I command you
today, that the Lord your God will set you high
above all nations of the earth. And all these
blessings shall come upon you and overtake you,
because you obey the voice of the Lord your God.
Deuteronomy 28:1-2

God then delineated the impressive list of blessings that
would "overtake" Israel, if they would live in faithfulness

to the covenant. The whole constitutional system was calculated to generate human thriving. If Israel would operate in harmony with the covenant, God promised they would be "the head and not the tail" in all their economic and political dealings. As a result, the Gentile nations would flow into Israel seeking the secret of their prosperity. The whole world would come to the knowledge of God through Israel's covenant witness (Deuteronomy 28:13; Isaiah 60:3; 66:12).

But alas, it didn't happen.

Israel chose monarchy over covenant as their preferred governing system, insisting that God give them a king so they could wage war like all the other nations (1 Samuel 8). Therefore, rather than attract the nations, Israel invited their hostility. In due course, they were a nation in captivity once again, this time under the rule of Babylon.

It is right here, against this historical backdrop, that we meet Daniel as a captive slave in Babylon and encounter his fabulous prophecies of a coming "Son of Man" who will become the long-awaited "Prince of the Covenant."

In Daniel's prophetic visions, a succession of four kingdoms is delineated:

Babylon

Media-Persia

Greece

Rome

As Daniel maps out the historical transitions from one kingdom to the next, he observes that each empire conquers the other by means of an escalating display of self-exalting power:

Triumphing over Babylon, Media-Persia "became great" (Daniel 8:4, KJV).

Triumphing over Media-Persia, Greece "waxed very great" (Daniel 8:8, KJV).

Triumphing over Greece, Rome "waxed exceedingly great" (Daniel 8:9, KJV).

Human governance is a perpetual cycle of force, and greater force, each empire operating by the same basic principle—the will to power by means of violence.

But the gospel (or good news) according to Daniel is that the anti-covenant cycle will be broken. A different kind of king will emerge on the scene of human history and establish a different kind of kingdom:

> I was watching in the night visions,
> And behold, One like the Son of Man,
> Coming with the clouds of heaven!

He came to the Ancient of Days,
And they brought Him near before Him.

Then to Him was given dominion and glory and
a kingdom,
That all peoples, nations, and languages should
serve Him.
His dominion is an everlasting dominion,
Which shall not pass away,
And His kingdom the one
Which shall not be destroyed. . . .

But the saints of the Most High shall receive the
kingdom, and possess the kingdom forever, even
forever and ever. . . .

I was watching; and the same horn was making
war against the saints, and prevailing against
them, until the Ancient of Days came, and a
judgment was made in favor of the saints of the
Most High, and the time came for the saints to
possess the kingdom. . . .

Then the kingdom and dominion,
And the greatness of the kingdoms under the
whole heaven,
Shall be given to the people, the saints of the
Most High.
His kingdom is an everlasting kingdom,

And all dominions shall serve and obey Him.
Daniel 7:9-27, KJV

The prophecies of Daniel are a study in contrast. We are
called upon to examine two diametrically opposite systems
of rule—that which is on display in Babylon, Media-Persia,
Greece, and Rome, on the one hand, and the kingdom of
the Son of Man, on the other. Daniel is, therefore, a book
of judgment—judgment *against* the power-mongering
kingdoms of this world and judgment *in favor* of the
kingdom of the Son of Man. More specifically, Daniel is a
book of judgment *against* the principles of self-exaltation
and force by which the kingdoms of this world rule, on the
one side, and judgment *in favor* of the principles of humility
and love by which the Messiah rules, on the other side.

According to Daniel's prophetic timeline, the Son of Man
emerges during the reign of the fourth kingdom, or the
Roman Empire. The dark genius of force reached its zenith
with the iron monarchy of Rome. From Britain to Africa the
fearful chant, "Caesar is Lord," was forced from human lips.
It was into this world, into the jaws of the most terrifying
military superpower the world had ever known, that Daniel
proclaims, "Behold, One like the Son of Man," and "to Him
was given dominion and glory and a kingdom."

Another kingdom?

Yeah, yeah, yeah, we know kingdoms. Been there,
done that.

But no, this kingdom is different. Rather than measure force against force, violence against violence, Daniel reports, to our utter astonishment, that "Messiah shall be cut off, but not for Himself," and in so doing "He shall confirm a covenant" (Daniel 9:26-27). Self-sacrificing love defines this unanticipated "King of the Jews." Standing before Rome, that colossal paragon of human power, He speaks with a deeper power, "Father, forgive them, for they do not know what they do" (Luke 23:34). He was not trapped. "No one takes it from Me," He stated, "but I lay it down of Myself. I have power to lay it down, and I have power to take it again" (John 10:18). There was no deep-seated violence in His character waiting to burst forth when brought under pressure. "Who, when He was reviled, did not revile in return; when He suffered, He did not threaten, but committed Himself to Him who judges righteously" (1 Peter 2:23).

Identifying Himself as "the Son of Man" foretold in Daniel's prophecy, Jesus, before His crucifixion, had carefully articulated the nature of His kingdom:

> You know that the rulers of the Gentiles lord it over them, and those who are great exercise authority over them. Yet it shall not be so among you; but whoever desires to become great among you, let him be your servant. And whoever desires to be first among you, let him be your slave—just as the Son of Man did not come to be served, but

to serve, and to give His life a ransom for many.
Matthew 20:25-28

Every empire of the world rules by means of the same
principle: "authority over" others. By infinite contrast,
the Son of Man steps on the stage of human history, not
to be served, but to serve, and to give His life for those
who would take it from Him. The Son of Man isn't merely
more powerful than the other kings, He is more powerful
with a fundamentally different kind of power. He isn't
merely stronger on a scale of magnitude, rather His power
is measured on an entirely different scale. The kings that
dominate the human landscape rule by sheer force of
might. Jesus rules by the sheer might of love. They take
their places seated upon thrones. He takes His place nailed
to a cross.

The "Son of Man" in Daniel's visions is also known as "the
Prince of the Covenant" (Daniel 11:22). He rules by means
of covenant, and covenant dictates an utterly different kind
of relational dynamic than that employed by the power
structures of our world. Covenant, as we have previously
noted, is a biblical word that describes what relationships
look like when they are governed by faithful love. Jesus
establishes His kingdom, not by force, but by self-sacrificing
love. His voluntary death on the cross is the irrefutable
proof that He alone is worthy to rule the world.

The whole point of Daniel's prophetic book is to paint a
picture of the contrast between the principles by which

the kingdoms of this world operate, on the one hand, and the principles by which the kingdom of Christ operates, on the other. Daniel's deep genius is that he presents the stark contrast between the *love of power* and the *power of love* as diametrically opposite governing principles.

We're simply not going to get from the Bible what it has to offer unless we start reading it as a whole and track with its narrative flow. Once we do so, we will begin to notice on every page that there are two principles contending for supremacy. Just two. Everything boils down to just two antagonistic motives. The great controversy between good and evil is a war between two diametrically opposed ways of living life and governing the world: the love of power versus the power of love.

In Daniel's framing of history, the principle of selfishness is embodied in the pride and violence that actuate the empires of our world. The principle of self-giving love, by contrast, is embodied in God's Messiah, the Prince of the Covenant, who submitted to our violence without retaliation. By that one epic act of love, Jesus set in motion the one and only counter-narrative known to humanity. At the cross, we see the masterstroke of history, the genius maneuver of the ages. Jesus "tricked" the powers of darkness by refusing to fight back as they took His life, thus keeping love intact in Himself to the point of death. His resurrection is proof of love's triumph over evil. The kingdom of Christ is eternally sustainable, not because He uses more force than any other kingdom, but because He rules without force and thereby draws His subjects to Himself without ever resorting to coercion. Jesus didn't come to merely *win* the game, but to *change* the game. He didn't come to simply exert *more* power than all other rulers, but to exert a *different* kind of power. He came to win the game on different principles and on a different level. He came to conquer evil by love alone, or not at all.

When the New Testament tells us that Jesus is "the Son of God," it is telling us that He is the new head of Adam's race. When the New Testament tells us that he is "the Son of Man," it is telling us that He now occupies the throne of the eternal kingdom as a full-fledged member of the human race in Adam's lineage. Through the kingdom-building work of the Son of Man, humanity has been reinstalled as the benevolent ruler of the world. By His covenant-confirming death on the cross, Jesus has conquered the usurping "ruler of this world" and returned the earth to human lordship. We see, then, once again, that the point of the biblical narrative is not that God would rule the world, but that God *as man* would rule the world. And to do that, the God of the universe condescended to become one of us, as Isaiah foretold:

> For unto us a Child is born,
> Unto us a Son is given;
> And the government will be upon His shoulder.

And His name will be called
Wonderful, Counselor, Mighty God,
Everlasting Father, Prince of Peace.

Of the increase of His government and peace
There will be no end,
Upon the throne of David and over His kingdom,
To order it and establish it with judgment
and justice
From that time forward, even forever. Isaiah 9:6-7

Isaiah has given us the whole story in a single
poetic microcosm:

A Child will be born to the human race.

A Son will be given to the world.

He will establish a government unlike all the other
systems of the world, for this Prince will be a Prince, not
of war, but of peace.

He will carry upon His shoulders the total responsibility
of setting up the new government, and it will last forever
because it will be established "with judgment and justice."

Who is this Son given to the human race?

Who is this revolutionary Prince of Peace?

Who is this King who will overthrow the violent regimes of the world without resorting to violence Himself, and thus be established forever upon the throne of David?

He is none other than "the Mighty God!"

The "Son of Man" in Daniel's prophetic vision is a king who represents a kingdom that stands in contrast to the empires of the world.

He is the agent through whom the world will be reorganized within the relational framework of covenant. Whereas Babylon, Media-Persia, Greece, and Rome—as well as every other kingdom of the world—operates on the premise of power, employing violence for the spread of their rule, the Son of Man achieves His rule by means of self-sacrificing love.

Daniel's visions reveal that the kingdoms of this world pass in review before God and are found wanting. The Son of Man steps forward and promises a different kind of kingdom. The earthly empires that rule by violence are judged by means of the contrast presented in Christ. His benevolent reign stands in judgment against the ruthless manner in which they reign. There is a logic of contrast embedded within Daniel's prophecies. The point is not that the Son of Man will simply conquer the other kingdoms, but that He will be a different kind of king who will usher in a different kind of kingdom. Yes, He will conquer all the empires of the world, but He will do so with a power that is foreign to their conceptions of power.

They rule by war, He by love.

They rule by taking, He by giving.

They rule by coercion, He by covenant.

"Jesus emerges in the biblical narrative as the one Man who is true to the human potential, true to the original ideal for which humanity was made, true to God's image. As such, He is the Son of God that Adam was supposed to be."

CHAPTER FIFTEEN

THE LAST ADAM

Okay, well, the book of Daniel just blew our minds, didn't it? Wow, what a breathtaking vision of the Messiah's mission! Now let's hear from the apostle Paul on the same theme, exploring his powerful insights in 1 Corinthians 15.

Whereas Daniel presents Christ as "the Son of Man" who will set up an everlasting kingdom unlike anything the world has ever known, Paul presents Jesus as the "last Adam," the final rendering of Man, through whom all the top-down systems of our world will be overthrown.

Now if that's not a provocative and tantalizing prospect, nothing is.

First, Paul wants us to understand that the gospel consists of a single historical event that acts as a microcosm of the new humanity—the life, death, and resurrection of Christ. This, Paul says, is "the gospel . . . by which also you are saved" (1 Corinthians 15:1-4). We will call this piece of history *the Christ event.*

The reason Jesus alone, as a self-contained historical occurrence, constitutes the gospel, is that by His life, death, and resurrection He didn't merely *offer* redemption to humanity, He fully *achieved* the redemption of humanity in Himself (Romans 3:24). He lived a perfect life of love, died for our sins, rose from the dead, and ascended to the throne of God—all as a human being. And, according to Paul, Jesus did not achieve all of this as just any human being, but rather as "the last Adam" who, in effect, replaces "the first man Adam" (verse 45).

Jesus is the prototype of a new human race.

Jesus is humanity 2.0, officially launched and available for download.

Jesus is the one human in whom all humans are now *represented*, and into whom all humans are now *invited* for the acquisition of a new identity.

Hypothetically, for the sake of making the point, consider this: even if every human being were to refuse the salvation achieved in Christ, humanity, right now and forevermore, occupies the throne of the universe. A specimen of the human race is already there, in the victory position at the right hand of the Father. So the gospel is good *news*, not good *advice*. It proclaims salvation as an already-accomplished reality in Christ, rather than what we must do to manufacture any additional aspects of that reality.

This is so amazing already, isn't it? And Paul is just getting started!

Next, Paul dives deeper into the implications of the resurrection part of *the Christ event*. He wants us to understand what the resurrection of Jesus means for each of us as individuals and, more to Paul's key point, what it means for all of us collectively as a world system.

Apparently, some individuals in Corinth were saying "there is no resurrection of the dead" (verse 12). So Paul is addressing that denial and, in the process, he lays down some amazing insights. He begins by insisting that the resurrection of Christ is a historical fact, based on the solid evidence of numerous eyewitness accounts. The risen Christ "was seen by over five hundred brethren at once," by "all of the apostles," and "last of all He was seen by me also" (verses 5-8). Then Paul explains the implications that naturally follow if Christ has not risen from the dead:

> But if there is no resurrection of the dead, then Christ is not risen. And if Christ is not risen, then our preaching is empty and your faith is also empty. . . . And if Christ is not risen, your faith is futile; you are still in your sins!
> 1 Corinthians 15:13-14, 17

"Faith" here is specifically centered in "the gospel"—*the Christ Event*—and its resulting remake of humanity. If Christ died, but He did not rise from the dead, Paul reasons, then we are "still in our sins." In other words, if Christ didn't achieve the complete rewrite of Adam's failed history, then sin is our final, irrevocable story. To be "still in our sins" in this context means to remain in the fallen identity of the first Adam, with no second Adam from whom we can be reborn toward a new identity. But Paul insists that Christ *is* risen from the dead, which means we need not remain in our sins. The gospel, then, while it is a past tense historical event, also has present-tense implications. The resurrection of Christ signals a new reality to which we can relate and with which we can engage, so that we need not remain in our sins.

When we are dislodged from the big story of Scripture, we see none of this. We come upon the words *salvation, faith,* and *sins,* and we think Paul is talking about something along the lines of, *Say the sinner's prayer in order to get saved so you can go to heaven when this life is over.* Maybe that's in the back of Paul's mind, but if it is, he doesn't tell us. What he does tell us is that the life, death, and resurrection of Jesus equates to a victory so mammoth in its scope that it has launched a new humanity. "Salvation" from our "sins" by "faith" within the parameters of *this* story, means identifying with Christ as our last Adam such that our stories become an expression of the story of His death and resurrection.

Yes, there is a heavenly life after this earthly one, according to Paul. "For the trumpet will sound, and the dead will be raised incorruptible, and we shall be changed. For this corruptible must put on incorruption, and this mortal must put on immortality" (verses 52-53). Yes, when Jesus returns, the dead in Christ will rise to immortality. But that future resurrection, Paul insists, rests on the premise that Christ has risen from the dead and therefore has achieved a victory that spawns a new Adamic identity from which to live our lives in this current world. If He is not risen, then our "faith is empty" and "futile," Paul says. It has no historical content for its grounds and therefore no practical implications for how we live. We know Christ *is* risen, though, because we are experiencing the positive outcomes of His resurrection by breaking ranks with our sins in this present life.

If Christ is not risen, Paul continues his line of reasoning, "then also those who have fallen asleep in Christ have perished. If in this life only we have hope in Christ, we are of all men the most pitiable" (verse 18-19). The resurrection of Christ is the seismic event of history that promises the resurrection of all who have died. So if His resurrection didn't happen, well, death is our final state, and this whole idea of Jesus rewriting the human script is false. However, Paul is certain the story of Christ is true and that the implications are massive:

> But now Christ is risen from the dead, and has become the firstfruits of those who have fallen asleep. For since by man came death, by Man also came the resurrection of the dead. For as in Adam all die, even so in Christ all shall be made alive. But each one in his own order: Christ the firstfruits, afterward those who are Christ's at His coming. 1 Corinthians 15:20-23

Christ *is* risen from the dead, Paul insists, and that makes Him "the firstfruits" of all those who shall "be made alive." Death came into the world through a man (the first Adam), so death had to be reversed through a man (the last Adam). Again, we see that the biblical narrative revolves around the idea that God will restore humanity *from the inside*, through a human being in the Adamic lineage. What we see happening in Christ is not God *as God* reversing the effects of Adam's fall, but God *as man* rewriting human history. This is the pervasive logic of the biblical narrative. Imposing on the story curiosities and concerns regarding the ancient ontological origins of Christ only serves to divert our attention from the real issue at hand—namely, that this person we call Christ is none other than the covenant-keeping God of the Old Testament, who has now entered into the human story by becoming the faithful Son of God that Adam was supposed to be.

It is within this narrative context that Jesus is elsewhere called, "the Beginning, the Firstborn from the Dead," and "the Beginning of the Creation of God" (Colossians 1:18; Revelation 1:5; Revelation 3:14). These titles have nothing to do with Jesus coming into existence as the first being created by God. Jesus is the last Adam and therefore the new starting point for creation. His resurrection as the Adamic Son of God signals the rebirth of creation. Once we take into account the Old Testament narrative, it is so obviously clear that this, precisely *this*, is what these titles for Christ mean. With the story of Scripture before us, there is simply no justification for insisting that these passages are talking about the ancient metaphysical beginnings of Christ. More tragically, when we fail to follow the story where it leads, we inevitably miss Paul's massively important punchline regarding *the Christ event*, to which we now turn our curious attention.

Because Paul is operating within the Old Testament narrative, with a clear vision before him of a Messiah who has embarked upon a mission to remake humanity, he goes on to announce the rather astounding and inevitable impact *the Christ event* will have on our world as a whole:

> Then comes the end, when He delivers the kingdom to God the Father, when He puts an end to all rule and all authority and power.
> 1 Corinthians 15:24

This is one of the most revolutionary declarations ever penned. Here we are told that the entire world system as we know it—the total psycho-edifice of human power structures—will come to an end as the final outcome of *the Christ event*. The life, death, and resurrection of Christ inaugurated a radically different arrangement of the world. If what Paul has written here is not true, the future of mankind is bleak beyond estimation. But if it is true, we are headed for the most glorious state of existence imaginable.

The first Adam and the last Adam present before us two diametrically opposed relational dynamics. The fall of the first Adam was a governmental fall as well as a moral fall. "God is love" and "God created mankind in His own image." Having created human beings in the image of His love, God gave them "dominion over the earth." Consider three self-evident truths that naturally follow from this narrative beginning:

1. The individual human self may be defined as a free agent in possession of the power to act toward others and thereby generate an endless cycle of novel relational outcomes.

2. Love may be defined as relational integrity in which the individual self acts with preference for the well-being of others before one's self, and sin may be defined as the abuse of power toward the hurt of others.

3. Therefore, all human relationships are power dynamics, and all power dynamics carry potential for either the abuse of power or the responsible employment of power.

At the core of Adam's sin was a fundamental misconception of power that led to a fundamental change in human power dynamics. Human beings were created *under* God and given dominion *over* the world. They were created *under power* and they were given *power over*—power, however, of a particular kind. The beauty of the arrangement lay in the imperative of love. Love is other-centeredness. Therefore, love may be defined as power exercised for the freedom and well being of others. This is the core reality of God's character and the premise upon which God operates in all relationships. Mankind's fall constituted a violation of love as the only viable and sustainable exercise of free moral agency. By introducing the principle of sin into the world, the first Adam set in motion a long, horrific history of human beings exercising power to the hurt of one another.

Male-female power dynamics, parent-child power dynamics, interracial power dynamics, corporate power dynamics, political power dynamics, economic power dynamics—in all of these relational systems we see reproductions of the fallen image of the first Adam. The last Adam has embarked upon a mission to destroy all abusive power dynamics and restore humanity to love-based power dynamics.

> Then comes the end, when He delivers the kingdom to God the Father, when He puts an end to all rule and all authority and power.
> 1 Corinthians 15:24

When we read these words, if we are attuned to the biblical narrative, our minds trace back to the vision cast by Daniel, and cast earlier by Moses, of a world governed by God's covenantal love and utterly free of all systems of abusive domination. Christ is the *Last Adam*, the *Covenant Man*, the *Definitive Human*, the *Final Man*. He is man as man was meant to be. As such, His task is twofold:

- save individual human beings from the distorted versions of themselves they have received as a legacy from the first Adam,

- and bring an "end to all rule and all authority and power," which has defined all the systems by which fallen humans run the world.

According to the biblical narrative, God is fundamentally against monarchy as a governing system. He explicitly told Israel so. He wanted to govern His people through prophets. Prophets are educators, not rulers. The goal of a prophet is to teach people the principles of covenantal living, toward self-governance. The goal of monarchy is to exercise power over people. The people insisted upon monarchy as their chosen system, so God accommodated their insistence while warning them of the dire outcomes (1 Samuel 8).

Within the biblical story, it is only after Israel institutes their monarchy that messianic prophecies begin to depict the coming Savior of the world as a King who will sit on the throne of David (2 Samuel 7:12-16; Psalm 2; Psalm 132:11; Luke 1:32). Then, when Jesus finally comes to our world to fulfill these prophecies, He completely reframes monarchy. The kingship role is radically refashioned in His hands. Jesus is an anti-King kind of King of an upside-down kingdom. As the people clamor for a king so they can wage war like all the other nations, Jesus essentially says:

You want a king? Okay, hand Me that apron and let Me serve you, because he that is greatest among you will be your servant (John 13).

You want a king to conquer your enemies? Okay, My kingdom will be populated with enemies that have been made friends by forgiveness (Matthew 5; Luke 23:34).

You want a king to rule over you? All right, enthrone Me on that cross and I'll draw you to Myself with love rather than drive you by force (Matthew 27:37; John 12:32; John 18:36-37).

The resurrection of Christ, Paul explains, constitutes the triumph that will ultimately achieve the remaking of the world on the premise of love rather than power, or, if you like, on the premise of love as the only real power. But we have largely missed this deep and profound truth that lies embedded within the resurrection of Christ as the last Adam. Because Christian evangelism has tended to reduce the Bible to an encyclopedic tool from which to construct doctrinal arguments, we've tended to overlook the larger contextual issues the biblical writers themselves are addressing. As a result, we've reduced the resurrection of Christ to a proof of His divinity.

Oddly enough, or perhaps not so oddly, the New Testament never presents the resurrection of Christ as proof of His divinity. Yes, He is God. And yes, His resurrection can serve as evidence of that fact. But that's

not the point Paul makes regarding His resurrection. The
resurrection of Christ, in Paul's understanding, is the
definitive evidence that the last Adam has finally come,
just as promised, and has triumphed over our world's
abusive systems of power and launched a new kingdom
that will inevitably render "all rule and all authority and
power" obsolete. Why? Well, because all such systems
violate the integrity of the covenantal identity of both God
and humankind. So, then, the last Adam is in the process
of executing the delicate mission of negating all earthly
power structures and bringing the world back "under
God" where it belongs:

> For He must reign till He has put all enemies
> under His feet. The last enemy that will be
> destroyed is death. For "He has put all things
> under His feet." But when He says "all things are
> put under Him," it is evident that He who put
> all things under Him is excepted. Now when all
> things are made subject to Him, then the Son
> Himself will also be subject to Him who put all
> things under Him, that God may be all in all.
> 1 Corinthians 15:25-28

Some use this passage as a prooftext, completely dislodged
from the story of Scripture, interpreting it to mean that
Jesus has always been subordinate to God the Father.
From that interpretive premise, they deduce that Christ
must, therefore, occupy an eternal position secondary to
the Father in both chronological existence and ontological

identity. But now that we are allowing the story of
Scripture to interpret all New Testament depictions
of Christ, it is evident that Paul is here describing the
deeds of Christ as the last Adam. An ancient hierarchical
subordination structure within the Godhead prior to
Creation is nowhere on Paul's radar. He is telling us,
rather, that Christ, as the new representative head of the
human race, is in the process of bringing the world back
"under God," including "the Son Himself," *as the new
Adam*. Jesus, the last Adam, is brought back "under God"
where He belongs, and where the first Adam was created
to be. According to the story Paul is working from, Adam
was created *under* God and placed *over* the earth, but he
forfeited that position by attempting to exalt himself to
equality with God, placing himself under a new ruling
lord, namely Satan. Jesus, as the last Adam, came to rectify
the situation.

But while nothing in this passage indicates an
ontological hierarchy within the Godhead in eternity
past, what it does tell us, astoundingly, is that Christ
will forever remain in the Sonship position as our new
Adam. This is a revelation of God's self-giving love
that boggles the mind. To think that this One who
had, for all eternal ages past, been nothing less than
pure, transcendent God, possessing all the prerogatives
that belong to divinity—omnipotence, omniscience,
omnipresence, and God only knows what else—laid all
that aside to enter into eternal solidarity with us, is a
wonder beyond comprehension.

God's purpose for humanity is that they rule *over* everything *under* God. Paul's discourse in 1 Corinthians 15 is all about how humanity, in and through Christ, is now restored to its rightful position of rulership *over* the world, *under* God.

The biblical narrative teaches us that there are only two ways to conduct ourselves as free moral agents:

- the power-*over* way or the power-*under* way

- the way of *domination* or the way of *peace*

- the way of *authority* or the way of *love*

And according to Paul's final rendering of the world, everything that operates by the oppressive exertion of power over others is coming to an end.

Freedom is necessary for the existence of love, and love is necessary for the ongoing existence of freedom. When we use our freedom for anti-love purposes, it vanishes and we become slaves to self-serving impulses. That's what the first Adam gave us. As the last Adam, Jesus is restoring to us the responsible exercise of our free agency, redeeming us from the lust for control, saving us from the will to assert self over others, and reintroducing God's love into all of our relational dynamics. He is transforming us back into beings who can hold power in reserve, in favor of the autonomy of others.

By introducing the principle of self-centeredness into the world, the first Adam forfeited his position of benevolent dominion over the world. The covenant of love was broken (Hosea 6:6-7, ESV; Isaiah 24:4-6). Satan became the "ruler of this world" and brought the world under his "sway" (John 12:31; 1 John 5:19). In light of this narrative, Paul comes along and preaches the gospel by telling us that Christ has inaugurated a process by which everything in the world is being brought "under His feet." But there is a deep and beautiful irony here: "under His feet" things are ruled by being served, not by being dominated. The last Adam's mission, according to Paul, is to regain dominion of the world, not in order to rule the world the way all the other rulers have, but rather to institute an entirely different kind of rule. He will bring an end to all despotic, coercive, violent systems of governance, and He will restore the principle of self-giving love as the only legitimate principle of governance. Paul is not portraying Jesus *as God* taking back the world from Satan's illegitimate rulership, but rather God *as man* regaining rulership of the world, that it might be ruled the way it was meant to be ruled—by covenantal love. Jesus is doing what He's doing as "the last Adam," which is to say, as "the Son of God." So when Paul says God has brought everything "under His feet," those are human feet.

It is none other than the Son of God, in Adam's line, who is on the move in the world.

It is the Son of Man, foretold in Daniel's prophecy, who is afoot among the sons of men, overturning all the power structures of the earth.

It is the Prince of the Covenant who is staging a benevolent takeover of the world, and His covenantal death is the definitive revelation of His character.

In Christ we see a micro-reenactment of history: the failure of the first man is redeemed by the last man.

In Christ we witness a grand reversal of roles: the powerful go down, and the humble are exalted.

In Christ we encounter a complete reframing of reality: love alone is the measure of greatness.

Jesus emerges in the biblical narrative as the one Man who is true to the human potential, true to the original ideal for which humanity was made, true to God's image. As such, He is the Son of God that Adam was supposed to be. Christ is our new Genesis. Creation is relaunched in Him. In principle, the recreative deed is done in Christ. Now the new human identity He achieved is to be replicated:

> The first man was of the earth, made of dust;
> the second Man is the Lord from heaven.
> As was the man of dust, so also are those who
> are made of dust; and as is the heavenly Man, so
> also are those who are heavenly. And as we

have borne the image of the man of dust, we
shall also bear the image of the heavenly Man.
1 Corinthians 15:47-49

The overt narrative logic of the New Testament reaches its
pinnacle here. "The second Man is the Lord from heaven"
(verse 47). God became human in order to reincorporate
humanity into the Sonship role we were meant to occupy.
"The Lord from heaven" has accomplished this by
becoming our new representative head, our last Adam,
God's true Son, first bearing and then reproducing God's
image, as was the plan from the beginning. So just as "we
have borne the image of the man of dust," if we choose
Christ as our new beginning "we shall also bear the image
of the heavenly Man" (verse 49). Before his fall, Adam
bore the "image of God" (Genesis 1:27). As the last Adam,
Jesus bore the "image of the invisible God" (Colossians
1:15). This is the grand point of His Sonship role. Paul is
not telling us that Jesus always was the Son of God, but
rather that "the Lord from heaven" *became* the Son of God
in order to restore the "image" of God in humanity. And
the restoration of that image, according to Paul, ultimately
involves the abolition of all abusive power dynamics and
authoritarian structures.

So we can let our imaginations run to the most beautiful
and inviting world imaginable.

Can you see it?

Imagine a world in which there is no self-serving hierarchy.

A world in which there is no dominance, but only shared dominion through reciprocal service.

A world in which relationships are not organized from the top down, but rather from the bottom up.

Imagine a world in which the top is the bottom and the bottom is the top, and nobody even cares to think about it.

A world in which everyone has forgotten about themselves while remembering everyone else.

A world in which the King is girded with an apron, washing feet and serving food.

Imagine a world in which the One who occupies the highest place actually prefers the lowest place.

A world, in fact, in which all of this language of high and low, up and down, top and bottom, is completely gone from consciousness and vocabulary . . .

except for the ceaseless, voluntarily exaltation flowing in praise from all rational creatures to the One and only true God, the eternal Three who are One in love.

It's almost impossible to imagine such a world because we fallen humans are addicted to the idea that power is equivalent to the exertion of control over others. Consequently, we have organized the whole world into categories of high and low, powerful and weak, rich and poor, free and bond, us and them. Our political systems, our economic systems, even our ecclesiastical systems, are all arranged in hierarchical form. But wouldn't it be amazing to live in a world in which all actions are simultaneously benevolent and free, and therefore absent all sense of control?

Well, just such a world is coming, and only those who serve the Son, who serves the God who serves those who serve the Son, will be part of it.

"Jesus is God's eternal
Son in the sense that He
was eternally pledged
to become one with
the human race and
fulfill the covenantal
terms of our Sonship."

CHAPTER SIXTEEN

ETERNAL COVENANT PLEDGE

So far in our survey of Scripture, we have seen that the New Testament writers view the Sonship of Christ as the outworking of the Old Testament story of Adam and of Israel. In their view, Jesus was begotten to the Sonship identity at the point of His incarnation. He is the Son of God in a narrative sense, in a covenantal sense, in solidarity with the human race. Once this larger biblical picture is seen, tremendous clarity is achieved with regards to the overall message of the Bible.

And yet, there is a natural question that arises at this point:

Is there any sense in which Christ was the Son of God *before* His incarnation?

Yes and no.

Yes, in the sense of an eternal covenant pledge made by God from the moment humanity was created.

No, with regards to His eternal, ontological identity before and apart from our creation.

Above and beyond all created things, and before the salvation enterprise was necessitated by the Fall of humans and angels, the One we now know as Jesus Christ was none other than God, very God, in His intrinsic eternal nature. And yet, Scripture sometimes speaks of Him as occupying the Sonship position prior to His incarnation. The question is, why? If Jesus was and is none other than eternal, underived, unborn, uncreated, infinite God, how can He be spoken of as the Son of God prior to actually being born into human nature via the womb of Mary? In this chapter, we will endeavor to answer this important and fascinating question. We will discover that God's covenant character carries natural implications for the way God operates in relation to all created beings. A magnificent truth will become clear with regards to the pre-incarnation Sonship of Christ:

Because God is love, God was eternally committed to becoming one with humanity in order to redeem Adam's Fall and rectify Israel's covenant failure. Our salvation was always upon God's heart as an "eternal purpose" (Ephesians 3:11). Therefore, the prophets spoke of the Sonship of Christ and of our redemption in Him as if it were an accomplished reality before the plan was fully carried out.

With that brief summary under our belt, let's dig in, starting with this crucial biblical revelation:

Our redemption was not an afterthought for God.

The apostle Paul describes human salvation as a plan to which God was committed even before the creation of the world:

> For I determined not to know anything among
> you except Jesus Christ and Him crucified. . . .

> But we speak the wisdom of God in a mystery,
> the hidden wisdom which God ordained before
> the ages for our glory, which none of the rulers
> of this age knew; for had they known, they
> would not have crucified the Lord of glory.
> 1 Corinthians 2:2, 7-8

> Blessed be the God and Father of our Lord Jesus
> Christ, who has blessed us with every spiritual
> blessing in the heavenly places in Christ, just
> as He chose us in Him before the foundation of
> the world, that we should be holy and without
> blame before Him in love, having predestined us
> to adoption as sons by Jesus Christ to Himself,
> according to the good pleasure of His will, to
> the praise of the glory of His grace, by which He
> made us accepted in the Beloved. Ephesians 1:3-6

> . . . the eternal purpose which He accomplished in
> Christ Jesus our Lord, in whom we have boldness
> and access with confidence through faith in Him.
> Ephesians 3:11-12

The crucifixion of Christ was "ordained before the ages"
as an "eternal purpose" residing in God's omniscient
mind. There is a sense in which we humans were chosen
"in Him before the foundation of the world." Then, at the
point of the incarnation, Jesus came and "accomplished"
our chosen status by becoming one of us, merging human
nature with the divine. Paul writes to Titus that we live "in

hope of eternal life which God, who cannot lie, promised before time began" (Titus 1:2).

"Promised."

Here Paul is operating within the matrix of God's covenant identity. The promise—the commitment, the pledge, the oath of God's eternal purpose to save humanity—was embedded within God's reality "before time began." This is an astounding statement on Paul's part, full of mind-boggling illumination. Before time began—whatever that means—the promise of God was intact within Himself. God's covenant is eternal in nature because it is grounded in God's very make-up as God. Love composes God's essential character, and covenantal commitment is what love looks like in action.

> "Though the mountains be shaken and the hills
> be removed, yet my unfailing love for you will not
> be shaken nor my covenant of peace be removed,"
> says the LORD, who has compassion on you.
> Isaiah 54:10, NIV

The "covenant of peace" is God's eternal pledge to save humanity at any and all cost to Himself. It is more likely for creation itself to unravel and cease from being than for God to stop loving us. Taking Paul and Isaiah together, we have a clear picture of God making a commitment, pre-Creation, to pursue fallen humanity and achieve our rescue by means of His unfailing love.

Also processing history within a covenant framework, the apostle John wrote that Jesus was "the Lamb slain from the foundation of the world" (Revelation 13:8). Of course, Jesus was not, in actual fact, slain from the foundation of the world. But He was "foreordained" to the performance of that task long before He actually carried it out at the cross. The one we now know by His human name, Jesus Christ, was covenantally promised to the human race before creation.

In the same manner, the prophet Isaiah foretells the sufferings and death of Christ as if the cross had happened before it actually did. Rather than saying, "He *will be* despised and rejected by men," Isaiah says, "He *is* despised and rejected by men." Rather than saying, "He *will* bear our griefs and carry our sorrows," Isaiah says, "He *has* borne our griefs and *carried* our sorrows."

In Isaiah's telling, the events of the cross had already occurred, and yet, in real time, they had not yet occurred. The attuned reader will notice that throughout the Old Testament the Messiah's mission is written *proleptically*, as if it were a present or past reality. *Prolepsis* is a common ancient and modern literary mechanism used to bring the reader vividly into the events described. To speak *proleptically* is to speak of something in the future as if it already existed or had occurred.

With God, love dictates all arrangements and outcomes. So the moment God said, "Let Us make man in Our image," God was prepared to keep on loving humanity, no matter where that love might lead. And where might that love lead?

Well, to the incarnation and to the cross!

To complete solidarity *with* and complete self-sacrifice *for* fallen humanity!

Therefore, following Paul's lead, we can say that the incarnation and the cross were potentiated in God's future from the moment He created others to share existence with Himself. The covenant of peace, or the promise God made in Himself before time began, involved a divine decision to form an intimate linkage between Himself and humanity. That linkage would become reality when God, in the person of Christ, would become the Son of God, or a full-fledged member of the human race.

Peter says it like this:

> He indeed was foreordained before the foundation of the world, but was manifest in these last times for you. 1 Peter 1:20

There is a clear chronological progression here:

> . . . *foreordained* before the foundation of the world . . .

. . . but was *manifest* in these last times . . .

. . . for you.

Creating free moral agents—beings with the capacity
for love—was a risky venture. With the freedom to
love, comes the freedom *not* to love, along with all the
horrific fallout entailed. God foreknew that the risk
factor inherent in creation would be realized in the
Fall of humanity, and He made provision for it. The
members of the Godhead entered into an agreement—
what the Bible calls a "covenant of peace" even "before
time began"—that one of them would be the medium
of communication between God and man. Therefore,
in a "foreordained" sense, it can be said with perfect
theological accuracy that Christ is God's *eternal* Son.
Eternal Sonship was embedded within God's eternal
purpose to save us. One of the Three was given to,
set apart for, and intimately intertwined with the
redemption of the human race, even before the world
was made. We can envision, then, that the covenant of
peace was and is the unfolding narrative within which
God has operated from the moment of creation forward.
As soon as God's love was actualized in the form of a
material creation, that creation was the center of God's
focus, passion, and organizational arrangements.

Once we grasp God's essential covenantal orientation,
we can easily understand why the visions of the prophets
portray the relational dynamics of heaven as operating

within the human story, with the Father-Son relationship already being enacted, even before the Promised One was born to the world.

The point is a simple one: as soon as God embarked upon creation, all of God's government, systems, posturing, and plans were set in motion for the purpose of communicating with and saving His creation. From eternity past, Christ was set up as the Son of God, as the one who would mediate all communication and perform all redemptive deeds on behalf of mankind. He was always covenantally pledged to the Sonship identity and mission. And yet, He did not actually become human, and thus God's Son, until the moment of His incarnation. Prior to His birth, for all eternity past, He was *already-but-not-yet* the "Son of God."

If I am in the Army, for example, I *am* a soldier in the sense that I am committed to engaging in soldiering activities if and when the time comes that I must carry out that role. While I am already enlisted, I may not yet have performed the activities the role entails. By virtue of my commitment to the position, however, I am called by the title that the role confers upon me, even while I have not yet performed in that role. Likewise, if I am named the Ambassador of the United States of America to China, I *am* the Ambassador while I await the need to engage in ambassadorship activities. I bear the title that the role entails even before I actually engage in any ambassadorship tasks.

Similarly, but on a grander scale, Scripture is clear that God was committed to the salvation of humanity before the Fall occurred, even before Creation, in fact. In this sense, that member of the Godhead we know as "Jesus" (His post-incarnation human name) was pledged to take on the role of God's Son within the human realm. But— and this is both basic and crucial—His commitment to become human and enact the Sonship role is not to be confused with His essential, eternal identity as none other than God. God, no less than God, consented to *become* the faithful Son of God we humans were meant to be. He was eternally promised to us as the One who would assume the Sonship position. He was "foreordained" to Sonship "before the foundation of the world," but then was "manifest" as God's Son "in these last times."

Taking the Bible as our source of information, it can be said with accuracy that Jesus is God's eternal Son in the sense that He was eternally pledged to become one with the human race and fulfill the covenantal terms of our Sonship. What cannot be said with biblical support is that the Sonship position defines His intrinsic nature before Creation and apart from the salvation enterprise. If humans had never been created and fallen into sin, God would never have taken on human form in the person of Christ.

And this brings us to a strategic place of understanding where we can now contemplate God, as God, apart from all that is not God.

"God possesses the sum total of all the characteristics of all God has made, while simultaneously existing in an ontological realm beyond all God has made."

CHAPTER SEVENTEEN

THE TRANSCENDENCE OF GOD

Each year I stand before a classroom full of new students and lead them through a simple exercise. I draw a large circle on the board. "This circle represents the whole universe," I explain. Then, in relation to the circle, I ask, "Where is God?"

The outcome is always the same. About half the students say, "Everywhere in the circle," and the other half say, "Outside of the circle."

Both are correct, of course.

God is everywhere within the material universe in the sense of omnipresence (Psalm 139). Pantheism says that God is present *in* all of creation, whereas the biblical idea of omnipresence says that God is present *to* all of creation.

But God is also outside of the circle in the sense that God made the material universe and therefore is not part of it in nature, in substance, in kind.

Everything we've learned so far in this journey of ours involves thinking within our finite realm as human beings. Now it will be helpful to remind ourselves of the self-evident truth of God's transcendence.

The word *transcend* means, "to be above, beyond, or independent of; to exceed or surpass."

Quite simply, because God is God, God transcends all that is not God. That is, in God's essential nature, God exceeds, surpasses, and exists without equivalency to, all creation.

God made matter, therefore God transcends matter. God is not synonymous with the things God has made, but rather exists independent of all that God has made. The moment God has been described on the human plane of reality, language has been employed that comes short of God's reality. All words, terms, categories, and nomenclature that arise in human consciousness are necessarily temporal and material and therefore can only approximate who God is. That which can be named, is not God as God is in God's ultimacy.

If God made it, God transcends it.

God *made* a world that operates and perpetuates by means of a system of material pro-generation, therefore God *transcends* all the categories of material pro-generation: male and female, father and mother, son and daughter. All pro-generation categories necessarily, by definition, describe beings that come into existence through sexual process. Man is to woman a sexual counterpart of procreation, and vice versa. Son and daughter are products of the procreation process. If God is eternally self-existing, it is immediately evident that God necessarily transcends all of the categories of pro-generation.

Why, then, does God present Himself to us in Scripture as Father (Deuteronomy 32:6; Isaiah 63:16; Isaiah 64:8), Mother (Deuteronomy 32:18; Isaiah 42:14; Isaiah 49:15; Isaiah 66:13), and Son (Matthew 17:5; John 3:16; Hebrews 1:5)?

The answer, in a word, is *love*.

God is love, and love, by its very nature, desires relationship. Love wants to be known. But how is an uncreated God, who transcends all material categories, to make Himself known to created beings, who only exist within material categories?

The answer, in a word, is *mediation*.

Mediation is the means by which a transcendent God builds bridges of understanding into the minds of material creatures. God is completely other than what we are. We are created beings. God is not. We are men and women, husbands and wives, sons and daughters. God is not. "God is not a man" (Numbers 23:19), Moses declares, therefore God is not, in God's innate nature, a father or a son, a mother or a daughter. And yet, because God is love, God chooses to enter into complete mediatorial communion with us. So, then, the Bible presents God interacting with His creation with a great deal of fluidity, manifesting Himself in whatever form He deems necessary in order to draw close to us and be known by us.

Sometimes in Scripture God presents Himself as a father, other times as a son, other times as a mother, other times as a lover, other times as an angel. God presents Himself to us in the form of a burning bush, a rushing wind, a descending flame, a dove, an eagle, the emblems of bread and wine. In a strict, ontological sense, God is not any of these creaturely or material realities. And yet, God is so humble and so eager to be known by us that He is willing to identify with us through the medium of these categories. God is none of these—neither male nor female, husband nor wife, mother nor father, son nor daughter— and yet God condescends to take on these kinds of roles in order to effectively communicate with us. Thinking through the entire realm of created things, Job mused about the fact that God transcends it all:

> Indeed these are the mere edges of His ways,
> And how small a whisper we hear of Him!
>
> But the thunder of His power who can
> understand? Job 26:14

God doesn't exist within our narrow, finite parameters. Rather, we exist within God's infinite parameters.

So, yeah, we don't know much—the mere "edges" or a faint "whisper"—by comparison to all there is to know about God. You know you're beginning to know God when you realize that you don't know much about God at all by comparison to the titanic reality of God's infinitude.

God doesn't float within the puddle that is creation. Creation floats within the massive ocean that is God's reality. There is a creaturely arrogance on display when an itty-bitty human being claims to know, within the limited parameters of material categories, that Christ began to exist at some point distinct from the Father as His ontological Son.

What!?

How could we possibly know any such thing—especially when nothing of the sort is revealed to us in Scripture?

God possesses the sum total of all the characteristics of all God has made, while simultaneously existing in an ontological realm beyond all God has made.

There is something of maleness in the character of God, or else God could not have made the male.

There is something of femaleness in the character of God, or else God could not have made the female.

God possesses the attributes of fatherliness and motherliness, therefore God has created fathers and mothers.

God even possesses the characteristics of childhood, and so God has made a world that includes sons and daughters.

God is all of this in one sense, and none of it in another sense. God is not any one part of the great whole of what we see on display in creation, and yet His mind is the fertile soil of infinite personhood and creativity from which all varieties of personhood and creativity have been derived.

Or, we could reason all of this through with a process of elimination.

If we strip away all material and pro-generative categories that compose reality as we know it, what do we end up with? If we eliminate all creation and procreation, what remains? In other words, what is the raw, necessary, essential, eternal, unalterable, and unmade thing that transcends all things that are made?

God.

Pretend you are Albert Einstein for a moment and engage in a thought experiment. In young Einstein's imagination, he rode a light beam on its trajectory through the universe, which formed the foundation for his theory of relativity. In our thought experiment, let's ride the light beam of reason and eliminate the very universe itself from existence.

Strip away all cosmological motion and gravitational force, expansion and contraction, heating and cooling.

Strip away all planets and solar systems and the process of photosynthesis.

Strip away all plant life with its reproductive morphology by means of stamen interacting with pistil.

Strip away all animal life with its procreative process by means of sperm meeting egg.

Strip away all fathers and mothers, sons and daughters, males and females, impregnation and birth.

Strip away all nations and languages, cultures and histories, all linear succession of events.

Stripe away all matter.

Now stand there for a moment in your imagination with everything gone, and ask yourself, what's left when nothing material is left? The answer you will naturally deduce is simply and profoundly this:

All there is, is God.

Which prepares our minds for the next logical question.

If, apart from all creation, all there is, is God, what, or who, is God?

And the answer you will be inclined to deduce in response to this question is the most marvelous and astounding realization of all:

God is love.

God is absolute other-centeredness.

Stripped down to God's pure Godness, God is perfect relational bliss.

Of course, we could opt for another answer to the question, namely that God, apart from all creation, is pure aloneness, isolation, and selfhood. But that's not only a bleak and ugly picture of ultimate reality, it's also unbiblical. According to the narrative that unfolds from Genesis to Revelation, God is love, and that means God, in God's pure Godness, is an eternal interaction of ceaseless love.

And with that, we are theologically equipped to grasp the relational genius that lies at the core of reality, so grab hold of your hat because now we're gonna fly into some extremely beautiful territory.

"To say God is love
is necessarily to
say that God is a
minimum relational
dynamic of three."

CHAPTER EIGHTEEN
THE GENIUS
OF THREE

So here's a weird question:

What is the minimum numeric value of love?

Or maybe it's not so weird, especially if you've ever been to high school and suffered the so-called "trauma" of being best friends with someone, only to have a third party enter the picture and threaten your egocentric bliss.

Or if you were ever floating along in matrimonial delight right up to the point when that new little human exited the womb and immediately took center stage in your lover's eyes.

Or if you ever had the rush of creative synergy with a colleague, only to have the whole thing disrupted by some new hire stepping into the room and capturing your colleague's attention with different ideas.

It's basically a relational geometry question.

Every year I pose the question to a class full of eager Bible students. Then I break them up into groups of two or three and tell them to discuss the question as they walk to the river. Upon arrival, there at the water's edge, I ask them to share the results of their conversations. It is always interesting—more like astounding—to hear their insights.

Why?

Well, because every year the same answer emerges, which indicates that our relational intuition as human beings is pretty uniform. We just know what we know, and we just happen to know the minimum numeric value of love.

First, the students easily rule out the number *one*. It is immediately obvious to everyone that love, by its very nature, cannot occur in isolation. Imagine one person existing alone in the universe, and you will find it impossible to imagine the existence of love. Love, by definition, is a relational dynamic, so if there were no other person with whom to relate, love could not happen.

Then the students banter back and forth with the possibility of *two* as the minimum number of people necessary for love to exist. A few students always begin by insisting that *two* is enough. "If love is other-centeredness," they reason, "all one person needs is one other person in order to experience love." But those insisting on *two* don't hold out long, because they sense there is some other mystery at work in the geometry of love. It's fun to watch them inch their way forward without any hints or help from me.

In every class, by the time we arrive at the river, there are a few discussion groups that are bubbling over with excitement as if they've had some major epiphany. And, in fact, they have. "*Three*," they insist, "it has to be *three*, a minimum of *three*. It could be more than *three*, but not less." Representative of what group after group has realized over the years, one student observed, "With just two people, no sharing of one another with anyone else is necessary, so you can easily be possessive and selfish. You need a third person in order to be selfless." One student after another jumps in with enthusiasm to articulate the relational genius of *three* as the minimum numeric value for a perfectly selfless love to exist. It really is very self-evident once the idea dawns. Think it through like this:

If there are two people, each one *has* an object for their love and each one *is* the subject of the other's love. But no sharing of each one's object of love is necessary. In order to experience a selfless sense of self, each one needs a third party to which attention may be deferred.

The massively popular 1969 Harry Nilsson song, *One*, touches on the absence of love from *one* and the challenge to love with just *two*:

> One is the loneliest number that you'll ever do
> Two can be as bad as one
> It's the loneliest number since the number one

If *one* is the loneliness number, and if *two* can be as bad as *one*, well, then, *three* may be the number that holds the secret of relational perfection.

One constitutes a complete absence of otherness.

Two constitutes a state in which each is the exclusive center of the other.

Three constitutes a state in which each one enjoys both being the center of attention and deferring the center of attention.

So three persons can experience giving love, receiving love, and expanding love to the level of third-party inclusion. The moment there are three, each recipient of love must also humbly yield love to the third party, and each one then occupies the position of the third party to the other two. Pure selflessness can now occur by virtue of the fact that each one must love and be loved with both an exclusive and a divided interest.

Or, think it through like this:

A conscious being is, by definition, self-conscious. One conscious being occupying existence alone could only experience self-consciousness.

If two conscious beings coexist, each one will experience three levels of consciousness: self-consciousness, consciousness of the one other, and consciousness of the one other's reciprocated consciousness.

But consider what happens when there are three persons. Three persons occupying existence together will experience an entirely different level of consciousness than that which is available to only two coexisting persons. Each of the three persons will experience self-consciousness, consciousness of each of the other two, consciousness of the other two persons' reciprocated consciousness, and consciousness of each of the other two persons' consciousness of one another, thus allowing each one to lose sight of one's self.

Got that? Haha!

In other words, in a relational unit of three,

- each one sees himself,

- each one sees the other two,

- each one sees the other two seeing himself,

- and each one sees the other two seeing one another.

And it is that last bit—the fourth state of consciousness—that places each of the three in the position of both *being* and *not being* the exclusive center of attention at any given point in the relationship. We can logically deduce, then, that a perfectly unselfish love can only occur with three or more individuals. It is self-evident that three persons compose the minimum relational dynamic within which a pure other-centeredness is conceivable.

The family unit is a reproductive phenomenon with a minimum relational dynamic of three: father, mother, child. And this minimal unit of three is defined in the creation account of Genesis as the "image" of God (Genesis 1:26-28).

I am not loved less by my wife because she loves our children, but more. I am not diminished in my capacity for loving my mother because I also love my father, and my mother would be misguided to think so. If you and I are friends, there is not less of you for me to love when we have a mutual third-party friend, but more. I am blessed to be loved by you, and I am blessed to share you with others and witness your love for them. I need to know you through another person's eyes, and through the activity of your relationship with others. Every two persons need at the very least a third person in order for each one to love on the level of knowing the second person from the standpoint of the third person. "You belong to me and I belong to you," needs to give way to, "and she's pretty amazing too."

So, then . . .

If God's essential identity is traceable to a state of solitary selfhood—*one*—which would be the case if Jesus in any sense had a point of beginning and if the Holy Spirit does not eternally exist with distinct personhood, then love is not essential to God's identity. If Father, Son, and Holy Spirit are not eternally co-existent, it cannot be said with any coherence that "God is love" (1 John 4:8).

When we say that God is God, the great I-AM-WHAT-I-AM, we are saying that, in the ultimate sense, God is completely other than anything within the realm of creation. At this level of perception, we can say three things about God:

God is love,

therefore God is an interpersonal relationship,

and that interpersonal relationship is necessarily composed of three persons, since love, to be perfectly selfless, must both receive and defer attention.

Beyond that, everything we say about God is metaphoric. Man, woman, father, mother, son, wind, dove, bread, flower, rain—whatever falls within the parameters of creation—are only penultimate approximations of God.

The most un-symbolic, non-metaphoric, ultimately literal thing we can say about God is that *God is love*. And when we say *God is love*, we mean that God is a perfectly self-giving social unit of three Persons who are one relational reality. Everything beyond this—everything material, temporal, and pro-generative—is the appropriation of language and forms to which we can relate and through which we can grasp different dimensions of God's love.

There is a pure, self-evident genius to the fact that the Bible identifies God as Three who are One, as a triune fellowship rather than as an absolute singularity, or even as a dualism. Scripture's revelation of God as a perfectly selfless relational unit of three is convincing evidence that the Bible is, in fact, the revelation of the one and only true God, whose essential nature is pure love. To conceive of God as three personal beings who exist as one is not an arbitrary construct, but rather it is inherently, intuitively, inescapably logical to the very outworking of the notion of love. What all of this means is that the Trinity isn't merely a philosophical idea imposed upon reality, but rather it is embedded within the very fabric of reality itself as we experience it. We *know* threeness is the minimum relational dynamic of love.

But let's take our exploration of *three* a step further for both fun and enlightenment, because it would seem that creation itself testifies to the number *three* as the essential numeric template of the divine character.

In 1970, a Soviet theoretical physicist by the name of Vitaly Efimov was doing what theoretical physicists do. He was working through some rigorous equations in his explorations of quantum mechanics. Along the way, to his surprise and amazement, his mathematical play yielded what appeared to be a rather strange characteristic of matter:

Trios of particles engage in arranging themselves in an infinite nesting-doll configuration.

Back in 1970, Efimov's idea was merely theoretical because he had only worked it out with equations on paper. Forty years later, over the course of about one month, three different groups of scientists, in three different countries, were able to create experimental environments that allowed them to actually observe Efimov's theory occurring in the quantum realm. What had been thought to be merely an outlandish idea, turned out to be true.

Cheng Chin, a physics professor at the University of Chicago at the time, enthused, "We are very excited about this result. In the complicated molecular world, there's a new law."

It might be called, *The Law of Trioism*, or in the words of senior science writer for *Quantum Magazine*, Natalie Wolchover, "The Rule of Threes." She describes the rule like this:

> The law is a geometric progression of evermore-enormous trios of particles, spanning in a theoretically infinite sequence from the quantum scale to (if the particles were cold enough) the size of the universe and beyond.

In other words, the entire physical universe displays a geometric tendency to organize into units of three on an infinitely expansive scale.

Visualize yourself opening an endless series of Russian Nesting Dolls. Each one you open reveals another, and yet another, and yet another, each one precisely the same in design. Now change the image in your mind from Russian Nesting Dolls to nesting triangles, or trios of particles, each geometric trio containing another, and yet another, and yet another, from the scale of infinitude to the infinitesimal level. Three, three, three, everywhere we look, a pattern of threes. That's what Efimov discovered. (You can watch a motion graphic of *The Efimov State* here: https://imgur.com/gallery/sUOV8). So it is fitting that this unexpected characteristic of matter is now called, *The Efimov State*, as a reminder that an obscure Russian physicist, playing with quantum equations, accidentally observed the nearly universal significance and inherent genius of the number three. And for those of us who believe that the physical universe was created by a supremely relational God, *The Efimov State* is also a reminder that the God who made it all is an interpersonal perfection of Three who are One. Bible students shouldn't be surprised at Efimov's discovery, because Scripture draws a clear line of correlation between the character of the Maker and the things the Maker has made:

> For since the creation of the world His invisible attributes are clearly seen, being understood by the things that are made, even His eternal power and Godhead. Romans 1:20

It logically follows that characteristics of the Creator would show up in creation. The whole material universe is math, math, and more math on all levels. Math is, in fact, the science of relationship, and relationship is the divine womb of all creation.

A science blogger named M. Mahin had an epiphany when he realized that "Nature loves the number 3" and "nature favors the number 3 in a deep and fundamental way." Mr. Mahin offered a series of examples, not the least of which is the fact that the entire material universe is constructed of building blocks that cohere as groupings of three in order to do their building work. He explains:

> First of all, there are three main types of stable particles: the proton, the neutron, and the electron. These are the three building blocks of atoms. All solid matter consists of atoms built entirely from these three particles.

> Scientists say that each proton and each neutron is built from smaller particles called quarks. How many quarks are there in a proton? Exactly three. How many quarks are there in a neutron? Exactly three. (http://futureandcosmos. blogspot.com/2014/01/nature-seems-to-love-number-three.html)

In other words, three is the minimum number of relational cohesion in subatomic matter. It would seem that the number three is God's mathematical signature written upon, or into, the physical creation.

We are thinking clearly when we reason like this:

1. God is love.

2. Love is a relational dynamic that requires a minimum of three persons.

3. Therefore God is a relational dynamic of three persons.

To say God is love is necessarily to say that God is a minimum relational dynamic of three.

"But what about the math?" someone will ask. "One is *one* and three is *three*, and it makes no logical sense to say there are three and then turn around and say there is only one God."

You are correct: the math doesn't make sense . . . if you never went beyond first-grade arithmetic.

1+1+1=3

But . . .

1x1x1=1

Each of the Three members of the Godhead combine to voluntarily disappear in the other two, rather than stand over-against the others. The math is not a problem for the Bible writers for the simple reason that they are not doing mere math. They're doing the relational dynamic of love. They are describing individual persons voluntarily canceling out self in order to prioritize others. To be and yet not be—that is the glorious mystery of love. The three persons that compose the oneness of the Godhead constitute an indivisible union in which each One constantly vanishes with humility in favor of the others and yet remains vital to the union.

And yet, a division did occur . . .

with excruciating agony.

That's where we need to go next.

"The obedience of Christ
to the point of death
was a supreme act of
covenantal faithfulness,
not a supreme act
of appeasement."

CHAPTER NINETEEN

CUTTING DEEP INTO GOD

Get three animals, cut each of them in two straight down the middle, and lay the pieces across from one another to form a pathway between the three sets of severed pieces.

Strange instructions, but that's what God told Abram to do. There was a context and there was a point, of course. A profound point. The most profound point that has ever been made in the entire history of point making, in fact. And that's no exaggeration, so let's not miss it.

God had recently made a big promise, the essence of which was that Abram and Sarai would have a son, who would have a son, who would have a son, generation after generation until, finally, a Son would be born through whom all the peoples of the earth would be blessed. Big promise, indeed. So Abram asked God how he could be sure the promise would be fulfilled. With this symbolic cutting ritual, God was answering the question. He was showing Abram what keeping His promise would ultimately entail. And, from the looks of the bloody, torn-apart carcasses on the ground, it would be a painful ordeal . . .

for God.

The day ended, the sun went down, and it became dark as Abram began to fall asleep, no doubt wondering what might happen next, because one thing was clear: the God of the universe was saying something. But what, exactly? Abram couldn't help but be curious. Suddenly, feelings of "horror and great darkness fell upon him" (Genesis 15:12). Abram was afraid of the future and he was struggling to believe God's promise. As the man lay there on the ground trembling with self-dependent anxiety, something happened:

> And it came to pass, when the sun went down and it was dark, that behold, there appeared a smoking oven and a burning torch that passed between those pieces. On the same day the Lord made a covenant with Abram. Genesis 15:17-18

The Hebrew word here translated "made" is *karat*, which means "cut." The word "covenant" is *berith*, which means "bond." When the text says "the Lord made a covenant with Abram," it literally means that God cut a bond or a covenant with Abram. *Strong's Exhaustive Concordance of the Bible* explains that *berith* is the word for "covenant" because "it was the custom in making solemn covenants to pass between the divided parts of victims." The ritual of cutting an animal in two and walking between the severed pieces communicated that a person was pledging their very life to fulfill their promise. Astonishingly, none other than God, in the form of a burning torch, walked the path between the severed pieces. God had made a promise to Abram, and now, with this ritual, He was telling the terrified man, *I pledge My own life for the keeping of My promise. I am willing to suffer and die in order to follow through with My love for you and all the peoples of the earth. I am a God who keeps covenant at any and all cost to*

Myself. There will be a great cutting, Abram, and it is God who will be cut.

But what kind of cutting are we talking about?

Within the realm of God's own divine reality—above, before, and beyond all of our material and reproductive categories—the three living persons of the heavenly trio have always existed in self-giving friendship. According to the covenant promise, all three members of the Godhead would endure the cutting necessary in order to maintain covenantal faithfulness toward fallen humanity.

Long after Abram was guided through the cutting ritual, the prophet Daniel was shown more explicitly that the symbolism would become reality when the Messiah would be—note the language—"cut off" in order to "confirm the covenant" (Daniel 9:26-27).

The covenant God made with Abram, and through Abram with the whole human race, was fully kept in Christ when He was voluntarily "cut off" from the Godhead. God's faithful love was "confirmed" when Christ was severed from the intimate fellowship that had defined the eternal connection of the three living persons of the heavenly trio.

And what a painful ordeal it was.

Imagine the pure bliss of God's eternal oneness. Imagine how completely immersed they were in one another's friendship. Imagine how deeply they were intertwined, each one with the others. Hold that nearly unfathomable image of perfect love in your mind for a moment . . . and then allow your imagination to grasp, if you can, the great cutting off from one another that the heavenly trio experienced. Try to comprehend, and even empathize with, the separating agony that ripped straight through the emotional core of God's eternal friendship.

The three personal Beings that compose the social reality that is God were split apart for love of you and me. Each of the three was torn in two within their individual emotional makeup as their blissful union was ripped apart. Humanity had failed to keep covenant, first in Adam, then in Israel. But rather than give up on us, grace welled up in the triune heart of God and we became the passionately pursued objects of a fierce love that would not let us go. In a vitally significant narrative twist, God would come to our world as the promised Son of God. God, as man, would keep covenant with God in order to redeem our failure and show us what love looks like in action. There is a lot at stake here for our comprehension of God's character. Reducing the Sonship of Christ to speculations about His metaphysical beginnings robs us of these rich insights into God's love that naturally unfold from the truth of God's triune oneness. But once we see God as an eternal relational union, the Christ event dramatically expands with clarity and beauty.

According to the story, the covenant cutting of God occurred in two vital phases of monumental sacrifice: the incarnation and the cross. Paul explains:

> Let this mind be in you which was also in Christ Jesus, who, being in the form of God, did not consider it robbery to be equal with God, but made Himself of *no reputation* (*kenoō*, the verb form of *kenosis*), taking the form of a bondservant, and coming in the likeness of men. And being found in appearance as a man, He humbled Himself and became obedient to the point of death, even the death of the cross. Therefore God also has highly exalted Him and given Him the name which is above every name, that at the name of Jesus every knee should bow, of those in heaven, and of those on earth, and of those under the earth, and that every tongue should confess that Jesus Christ is Lord, to the glory of God the Father. Philippians 2:5-11

Paul begins at the truly ontological level of Christ's identity, telling us who He always was before He showed up on earth. "Being in the form of God," Paul says, He was "equal with God."

Then Paul tells us that this one who was in very nature God voluntarily endured the most astounding alteration of His personhood imaginable: God underwent *kenosis*. The King James Version is deficient here by translating

kenosis, "no reputation," as if He merely underwent a
change in His external position in the eyes of onlookers,
rather than undergoing a change in His actual being.
The New International Version is better here, translating
kenosis, "He made Himself *nothing*." Still, though, the idea
is not fully achieved. The English Standard Version gets
to the real point of *kenosis* by telling us that He "*emptied
Himself*." This is the best translation because *kenosis*
entails the idea of contents being poured out. The Phillips
translation says Christ emptied Himself of His divine
"privileges" and "advantages."

Prior to His incarnation, this one whom we know by His
human name and title, "Jesus Christ," was one of the three
divine Persons of the heavenly trio. As such, He was full of
content that belongs by nature to God:

omnipotence

omniscience

omnipresence

Kenosis tells us that Jesus in some unfathomable sense
voluntarily submitted Himself to the limitations of human
nature. He never ceased to be God and therefore He never
ceased to have the freedom to use His personal omni-
powers. But He exercised what can only be regarded as an
infinite self-control, moved by an infinite love, to refrain
from using His divine powers for His own benefit, nor to

transcend the sense of separation from the Father that He endured in Gethsemane and at Calvary on our behalf.

He emptied Himself of omnipotence. Declaring His now dependent state, Christ said, "I can of Myself do nothing" (John 5:30). Assessing the display of miraculous power in His life, Peter said, "Men of Israel, hear these words: Jesus of Nazareth, a Man attested by God to you by miracles, wonders, and signs which God did through Him" (Acts 2:22). Clearly, the power we see on display in Christ is the power of the Father flowing through Him as His human Son.

He emptied Himself of omniscience. Having been born to Mary, Luke's Gospel informs us that "Jesus increased in wisdom and stature" (Luke 2:52). In other words, He learned things He did not know. Even in His adulthood, Jesus said that He did not know the time of His second coming: "But of that day and hour no one knows, not even the angels in heaven, nor the Son, but only the Father" (Mark 13:32). Clearly, by becoming a human being, Jesus dispossessed Himself of personal omniscience.

He emptied Himself of omnipresence. He said to Mary, "Do not cling to Me, for I have not yet ascended to My Father" (John 20:17). Clearly, He was not simultaneously present with the Father as He was present with Mary.

Even in His incarnation, Jesus was fully God. Therefore, He could have exercised His personal omnipotence, omniscience, and omnipresence at will, but he voluntarily emptied Himself, moment by moment, choice by choice, of the employment of His omni-powers for His own benefit. When Satan tempted Him in the wilderness, "If You are the Son of God, command that these stones become bread," Jesus didn't say, "Actually, Satan, that's a lame temptation because I can't even do that" (Matthew 4:3). Rather, He resisted the temptation by quoting Scripture. Apparently, if He chose to, He could have turned the stones to bread. This is a powerful microcosm of the entire *kenosis* process of the Savior's earthly life. Fully God, He could have exercised His God powers at any moment, but, moved by a love more powerful than all self-interest, He chose not to exercise those powers for Himself, choosing rather to rely on God as the first Adam should have done.

By making use of the Greek word *kenosis*, Paul wants us to understand that God was of such a "mind" (character, disposition, attitude) that He voluntarily "emptied" Himself of His natural God-abilities in order to embark upon the colossal enterprise of our salvation. So, then, the incarnation was not merely a change of geographical location for God, but rather a change of nature. He who had only ever been in very nature God, became in very nature human, His divinity retained, but now veiled in humanity. One of the members of the heavenly trio literally became a member of the human race. God became the Son of God.

This brings us to the second phase of the covenant cutting of God—the death of Christ on the cross of Calvary.

In Paul's thinking, God became human so that He might achieve something specific in our flesh. The incarnation was the necessary prerequisite to the cross. He submitted Himself to the limitations of human nature precisely for the purpose of becoming "obedient to the point of death, even the death of the cross."

Obedience?

What does obedience have to do with it?

Well, again, the truth of Scripture belongs only to those who take in the whole narrative. Only when we take into account the backstory to Paul's thinking can we possibly know how the cross constituted the climactic act of obedience necessary for our salvation.

Whereas every human son of God before Christ succumbed to Satan's temptations under lesser pressures—from Adam to Israel, from David to you and me—Christ followed through to remain faithful as the Son of God, even to the point of death. No degree of pressure could push Him to choose self-preservation over obedience to the "covenant" He came to "confirm" (Daniel 9:26-27).

Faithful love to God and to humanity was maintained in Christ, even in the face of total self-annihilation!

Faced with the prospect of being completely "cut off" according to the covenant contract made with Abram,

Christ chose all others over Himself. The "obedience" of Christ to which Paul refers is the covenant faithfulness to which all humans have always been called. At the cross of Calvary, we encounter God stripped naked to the essence of the divine identity. In the cry of dereliction, "My God, My God, why have You forsaken Me," all that remains is pure self-sacrificing love. Hanging there alone— God alone without God for the first time ever in all of eternity—we are face-to-face with a God who literally loves all others above and before Himself. In that one colossal act of perfect relational fidelity, Christ "confirmed the covenant."

Then comes Paul's punchline.

It was exactly on the premise of Christ's obedience to the point of death that He was rightfully and legitimately "exalted," and "given" a "name which is above every name."

What's happening at this point in Paul's reasoning?

Well, when Paul says that Christ was "exalted" as "Lord," he is simply following through with the biblical narrative by placing a human being, as the Son of God, upon the throne. The life, death, resurrection, and ascension of Christ was the life, death, resurrection, and ascension of the Son of God in the Adamic, Abrahamic, Davidic sense. By stepping down from His position of equality with God, becoming a member of the human race, voluntarily emptying Himself of His divine powers, and living in obedience to the covenant of love to the point of death, the position of rightful Lordship over the world that was lost by Adam was regained in Christ. Through Him, we are made sons of God once more, and the world is brought back under human stewardship.

The point of the New Testament is not that God, *as God*, is taking back the world, but that God, *having become human*, is taking back the world. Sonship is a human vocation, not a divine one, but a human vocation that God took up on our behalf. The Sonship of Christ is not His inherently divine identity, but His assumed human identity in solidarity with us. In Philippians 2, Paul is not trying to tell what God has done *as God*, but rather what God has done *as man*. The point of the passage is that we are to "let this mind be in [us]" that we see on display "in Christ Jesus." When Jesus died on the cross—victorious over self-centeredness and risen to the throne of the universe—He did so *for* us and *as* us. Jesus lived and died as our new representative head, as our new Adam. For the apostle Paul, then, the death, resurrection, ascension, and enthronement of Christ was the death, resurrection, ascension, and enthronement of humanity in Christ.

> Therefore, as through one man's offense judgment came to all men, resulting in condemnation, even so through one Man's righteous act the free gift came to all men, resulting in justification of life.
> Romans 5:18

I have been crucified with Christ; it is no longer I
who live, but Christ lives in me; and the life which
I now live in the flesh I live by faith in the Son
of God, who loved me and gave Himself for me.
Galatians 2:20

For the love of Christ compels us, because we
judge thus: that if One died for all, then all died.
2 Corinthians 5:14

God, who is rich in mercy, because of His great
love with which He loved us, even when we
were dead in trespasses, made us alive together
with Christ (by grace you have been saved),
and raised us up together, and made us sit
together in the heavenly places in Christ Jesus.
Ephesians 2:4-6

For if we died with Him, we shall also live
with Him. If we endure, we shall also reign
with Him. 2 Timothy 2:11-12

A Son of God, in the likeness of Adam, now occupies the
throne of the universe. He is there on our behalf, having
secured our place, awaiting our arrival. He holds before
us the astounding promise, "To him who overcomes I
will grant to sit with Me on My throne, as I also overcame
and sat down with My Father on His throne" (Revelation
3:21). "Do not fear, little flock, for it is your Father's
good pleasure to give you the kingdom" (Luke 12:32). In

Christ, humanity has returned to its rightful position of enthronement and covenantal reign over the world.

According to *this* narrative, the death of Jesus on the cross was not a sacrifice of the pagan kind, but of the covenant kind, reaching back in the story for its meaning to the cutting ritual God enacted with Abram. The obedience of Christ to the point of death was a supreme act of covenantal faithfulness, not a supreme act of appeasement. By allowing Himself to be cut off from the Godhead, He remained true to the ancient promise. In that one monumental deed of self-sacrificing love, relational integrity was achieved in all directions—God to man, man to God, and man to man—and human lordship over the world was reestablished in Christ.

"As we give ourselves over to the personal internal communion of the Holy Spirit, we are gradually, incrementally cultivated toward responsible self-governance until, at last, love alone defines every free act we perform."

CHAPTER TWENTY
THE UNFORCER

In Christ, the covenant sacrifice was made. God's faithful love was proven true. Within the realm of human nature, as the offspring of the woman, Christ became the new corporate head of the race. By this astonishing and incomprehensible act, God entered into eternal solidarity with humanity. Complete relational integrity was achieved as an objective, historical reality. The covenant of love was confirmed.

And this is where the Holy Spirit figures into the biblical narrative.

In the interest of achieving maximum clarity, I'll approach the exciting work of the Holy Spirit with a series of repeat-and-enlarge formulations. This will be super fun and enlightening, so give your whole mind and heart to the journey.

First, let's pan way out.

As we've already discovered, there are essentially two primary causal events that occur on the biblical stage. These two events define human history:

- the creation and the fall of the first Adam

- and the incarnation and redeeming work of the last Adam

In the largest of brush strokes, the creation account of the Old Testament is recapitulated in the redemption account of the New Testament.

In the Old Testament, God created mankind in His own image—to love like God loves, as a social community of relational integrity, to live in covenantal faithfulness toward God, toward one another, and toward the earth. The fall of humanity was essentially constituted in the breaking of the covenant of love.

In the New Testament, humanity has been and is being remade in the image of God, first in our new covenant head, Jesus Christ, and then in the new covenant community called the church.

This is what's going on in the story of Scripture.

This is the plot, the scheme, the point of the book. This is the grand narrative into which all the prophecies and stories feed. Therefore, we can expect that the narrative features that define the first creation will naturally show up in the re-creation. Sure enough, this is exactly what we do find to be the case. And the Holy Spirit is conspicuously present in both accounts, as we are about to discover.

Now let's pan in a little closer.

The Old Testament opens with the words, "In the beginning," followed by various narrative elements.

The New Testament, in John's telling, opens with the same words, "In the beginning," followed by the same narrative elements we find in Genesis.

The parallel is deliberate. One of the striking features of John's Gospel is that it is a redemptive retelling of the Creation story. By opening with the words, "In the beginning," John is triggering the old story in order for us to be in the right frame of reference to make sense of the new story. Let's notice how the comparisons line up.

In Genesis:

- "Darkness" covers the earth.

- "The Spirit of God" hovers or sweeps like wind "over the face of the waters."

- "Then God said . . . Then God said . . . Then God said . . ." The word of God is the active agent in the Creation event.

- "Light" illuminates the darkness by the active word.

- On the sixth day, mankind is created of "dust" (or flesh) and receives the divine "breath of life."

- Adam and Eve are given dominion over the earth.

- Adam and Eve are given power to procreate others in their image.

- The creation process is called "work" and God "finished His work" and "rested" on the "seventh day."

In John's Gospel:

- "Darkness" covers humanity.

- The "Word" of God is the active agent.

- "Light" overcomes the "darkness."

- The "Word" becomes "flesh" and receives "the Holy Spirit" at His baptism, as Adam was made of "dust" and received the "breath of life" at Creation.

- Jesus proceeds to demonstrate that He has "dominion" over creation, as the first Adam was meant to have, by commanding nature and engaging in a series of healing acts that indicate the reversal of the curse that was imposed upon the world by the fall of the first Adam.

- Jesus gives other human beings the "power to become the sons of God" in His image, taking up Adam's failed role to procreate children in his image.

- The process of redemption is called "work" and Christ "finished" the work on the sixth day when He died on the cross, and then rested on the seventh day in the tomb.

Wow!

All that's there, isn't it?

Yes, it is.

And unless we begin reading the Bible on its own terms—for what the Bible itself intends to convey in its own unfolding narrative—we will continue to prooftext ourselves into theological contradictions. But if we simply let the Bible have its way with us, we won't have to do a whole lot of interpreting, because the story will tell us what it wants us to know and will leave us with mystery in areas that are beyond the scope of the story and beyond our finite human grasp.

So far what we've seen is that Jesus is the Adamic "Son of God" reconstituted. In the gospel story, we are witnessing nothing less than the re-creation of the world through the redemptive work of Christ. Let's pan in closer now to observe more specifically the part the Holy Spirit plays in the story.

In the Creation account of Genesis, the Holy Spirit moves like wind on the waters, and the created world emerges from the waters:

> The earth was without form, and void; and
> darkness was on the face of the deep. And the
> Spirit of God was hovering over the face of the
> waters. Genesis 1:2

In the re-creation account of John, again the Holy Spirit
is associated with water and wind, and the new creation
emerges from the water:

> Jesus answered, "Most assuredly, I say to you,
> unless one is born of water and the Spirit, he
> cannot enter the kingdom of God. That which is
> born of the flesh is flesh, and that which is born of
> the Spirit is spirit. Do not marvel that I said to you,
> 'You must be born again.' The wind blows where
> it wishes, and you hear the sound of it, but cannot
> tell where it comes from and where it goes. So is
> everyone who is born of the Spirit." John 3:5-8

When Jesus insists that human beings must be "born of
water and the Spirit," He is invoking the Genesis account
of Creation and the role the Holy Spirit played in it.
The original Creation came forth from the water by the
movings of the Holy Spirit and speaking of the Word,
and now the new creation will be brought forth from
the water under the movings of the Holy Spirit and the
speaking of the Word. Jesus is conscious of His identity
as the new beginning of a new creation. He knows He is
the new Adamic Son of God who will now engage in a
procreative process of birthing many other children of

God. It is also clear that Jesus is telling us that the Holy
Spirit is intimately involved with Him in the re-creation
venture—so intimately involved, in fact, that as the story
continues to unfold we discover that the Holy Spirit takes
up a unique fellowshipping residence *within* human
consciousness, as breath fills the human body. Track
closely with me now as we pan in even closer, because this
is about to get really exciting.

The story of the Bible begins with a massively
charged breath:

> The Lord God formed man of the dust of the
> ground, and breathed into his nostrils the breath
> of life; and man became a living being. Genesis 2:7

Fast-forward to the New Testament, and Jesus closes His
earthly ministry with another massively charged breath:

> He breathed on them, and said to them, "Receive
> the Holy Spirit." John 20:22

The parallel is deliberate. In fact, the entire New
Testament is informed by the Old Testament, as we've seen
over and over again. What we see happening here is that
Jesus is drawing a parallel between the original breath of
life breathed into humanity and the new breath of life that
will define the new creation. He is telling us that the Holy
Spirit is the active, animating agent of the new creation, as
was the case in the original Creation.

The reason I say the breath of life breathed into Adam was *massively charged*, is because it is evident in the narrative that the original act of creation involved more than God merely blowing air into Adam's nose in order to get his lungs pumping. The lifeless form became a "living being." Something that was in God was now "breathed" into the physical shell lying there on the ground, and it was more than oxygen. It was, in fact, "the breath of *life*." When Adam began to breathe air, he also began to think thoughts and feel feelings. He began to consciously process the world around him as an autonomous being with self-awareness and awareness of others, which is to say, with the capacity for love. He became a living person with all the mental powers entailed in the wonder of existing as a "living being" animated with "the breath of life."

On the one hand, there is the physical body, composed of particles of matter. On the other hand, there is the spirit, the character, the breath of life, the personal identity of each human being. When a person dies, the particles of matter that compose the body decompose in the earth. But the breath of life—the spirit, the character, the personal identity—returns to God in an unconscious form to be preserved for the resurrection, at which point each one will receive an entirely new body. Scripture says it like this:

> Then the dust will return to the earth as it was,
> And the spirit will return to God who gave it.
> Ecclesiastes 12:7

Said less poetically, when a person dies, the physical body decomposes in the earth, and the spirit—the breath of life, including the individual identity—returns to God to be preserved for the resurrection.

So at the most basic level, human nature consists of two dimensions:

1. the body—the physical matter that composes the flesh-and-blood machine

2. the spirit—the personal identity with all the mental, emotional, and volitional components that define the individual character

But there is something more to the composition of the human being than the flesh and the spirit. In his sermon to Job, Elihu said there is a vital connection between the breath of life that animates the human being and the life-sustaining power of the Holy Spirit:

> The Spirit of God has made me, and the breath of the Almighty gives me life. Job 33:4

> If He should gather to Himself His Spirit and His breath, all flesh would perish together, and man would return to dust. Job 34:14-15

At the moment that Adam became a living being, he both possessed a spirit and was possessed by the Holy Spirit, creating a state of communion between the human and the divine. In other words, the human being is, by design, a habitable creature, and the Holy Spirit is the inhabitant we were created to host.

Pharaoh saw Joseph as "a man *in whom* is the Spirit of God" (Genesis 41:38).

Paul describes the followers of Jesus as "an habitation of God through the Spirit" (Ephesians 2:22, KJV).

The human being is a kind of house, a temple, for the indwelling of the Holy Spirit. "Do you not know," Paul asks, "that you are the temple of God and that the Spirit of God dwells in you?" (1 Corinthians 3:16). "Or do you not know that your body is the temple of the Holy Spirit who is in you, whom you have from God, and you are not your own?" (1 Corinthians 6:19). When, by their persistent choice, human beings expel the Holy Spirit from themselves, they finally "become the habitation of devils" (Revelation 18:2, KJV).

I am an "habitation."

So are you.

Vacancy is not an option for us humans.

We are not solo creatures, but rather communal creatures. We are either occupied by the Holy Spirit or, well, the alternative is downright scary. If occupied by darker inhabitants, our individuality is gradually canceled out until fully obliterated. If occupied by the Holy Spirit, on the other hand, our individuality is maintained and nurtured into a fully flowered state of free personhood. So Paul says, "Where the Spirit of the Lord is, there is liberty" (2 Corinthians 3:17).

The human being is a kind of house, or temple, for the indwelling of the Holy Spirit. The Holy Spirit's role in the re-creation, or the plan of salvation, is to take up fellowshipping residence inside the human person. Why, and to what end?

For our liberty!

For each one's restoration to one's best self!

More specifically, for the restoration of covenantal identity to humanity!

The new covenant is, by definition, the restoration of voluntary love in the human soul, moving God's law from the realm of externally imposed rules to the realm of internally embedded identity. And the Holy Spirit is the active agent of the covenant:

> I will give you a new heart and put a new spirit within you; I will take the heart of stone out of your flesh and give you a heart of flesh. I will put

My Spirit within you and cause you to walk in
My statutes, and you will keep My judgments and
do them. Ezekiel 36:26-27

If there is one thing Almighty God does *not* want, it's
control. Domination is contrary to the divine character.
God is not that kind of God. The grand objective of
creation, as we've seen, is that humanity would exercise
"dominion" over their own realm of existence in voluntary
harmony with God's character. This high state of being
was lost by means of Adam's fall. The plan of salvation is
the process by which humankind is restored to its proper
selfhood, to covenant-actuated living.

In Hebrews 10 we are told that there is a vital connection
between the work of Christ and the work of the Holy
Spirit. Christ's job in the salvation enterprise was to come
into our world and make the covenant sacrifice—that
is, to prove by His death that God's love is faithful, even
in the face of our sins. The covenant was confirmed by
"the offering of the body of Jesus Christ once for all"
(Hebrews 10:10).

But this Man, after He had offered one sacrifice
for sins forever, sat down at the right hand of
God, from that time waiting till His enemies are
made His footstool. For by one offering He has
perfected forever those who are being sanctified.
Hebrews 10:12-14

The Holy Spirit then proceeds to take up the task of
testifying to us of the covenant sacrifice and to work
within us to make its application to our lives:

> But the Holy Spirit also witnesses to us; for after
> He had said before, "This is the covenant that
> I will make with them after those days, says
> the Lord: I will put My laws into their hearts,
> and in their minds I will write them," then
> He adds, "Their sins and their lawless deeds I
> will remember no more." Now where there is
> remission of these, there is no longer an offering
> for sin. Hebrews 10:15-18

The Holy Spirit "witnesses to us."

Concerning what, exactly?

Concerning the revelation of God's faithful love given
to the world in Christ. Jesus made the covenant sacrifice
that reestablished self-giving love as the vital relational
dynamic between God and humanity, and the Holy Spirit's
job is to testify to that sacrifice, or to magnify God's love
in our understanding.

The same pattern of thought is worked out by Paul
in Romans:

> Now hope does not disappoint, because the love
> of God has been poured out in our hearts by the

Holy Spirit who was given to us. For when we
were still without strength, in due time Christ
died for the ungodly. For scarcely for a righteous
man will one die; yet perhaps for a good man
someone would even dare to die. But God
demonstrates His own love toward us, in that
while we were still sinners, Christ died for us.
Romans 5:5-8

Notice it is the special work of the Holy Spirit to flood our
hearts with awareness of God's love as it was demonstrated
in the self-sacrificing life and death of Jesus on the cross.
And then Paul follows up with this: "For as many as are
led by the Spirit of God, these are sons of God" (Romans
8:14). We become "sons of God," as we were created to be,
when we allow ourselves to be "led by the Spirit of God."
Led where, exactly? Into the love of God, Paul says. Why
is the love of God so important? Because, love and love
alone defines what it means to be in covenant relationship
with God and one another. Love defines, in fact, what it
means to really be human.

Okay, now watch this.

Because the Holy Spirit is the active agent of the
new covenant, and because the new covenant is the
reestablishment of God's love in the human person, the
work of the Holy Spirit is to be perpetually engaged in a
process of testifying without forcing, witnessing without
violating, communicating without coercing, carrying out

the delicate task of persuasion within our thinking and feeling process. It is the gingerly operation of saving us from sin while leaving the dignity of our free will intact and preserving the glory of our individuality. So, then, the work of the Holy Spirit is consistently depicted as one of *influence* as opposed to *force*. The Holy Spirit engages in:

Teaching (John 14:26).

Comforting (John 14:27).

Convicting (John 16:8).

Guiding (John 16:13).

Revealing (John 16:14).

Testifying (Romans 8:16).

Witnessing (Hebrews 10:15).

Inspiring (2 Peter 1:21).

Striving (Genesis 6:3).

Fellowshipping (2 Corinthians 13:14).

It is not by accident that all of these descriptors of the Holy Spirit are communicative and personal rather than coercive and impersonal in nature. The Holy Spirit is the member of the Godhead who completes the covenant loop between God and human beings, and between human beings with one another. That means the Holy Spirit's job is to generate a voluntary response within the human being. Within the scope of the biblical narrative, the Holy Spirit first "moves upon the surface of the water" like wind, and then moves within the inner landscape of the human mind as an intelligent, wooing, convicting, teaching, persuading communicator of the covenant. A Spirit-to-spirit communion is established within the realm of human consciousness.

So here's the thing that is now obvious: according to the biblical narrative, the Holy Spirit occupies the role of the internal communicator with whom human beings have communion. Therefore, it is completely inconceivable that the Holy Spirit would be an impersonal force. The anti-Trinitarian advocate will respond by saying something like, "Well, the Holy Spirit is a personal being, just not a *distinct* personal being from the Father and the Son, but rather the Holy Spirit *is* the Father and/or the Son." But this philosophical maneuver simply doesn't work within the biblical storyline for the following very simple reason. According to the narrative,

the Father is doing something,

through the person of Jesus,

to which the Holy Spirit testifies in our hearts.

That's the story, regardless of whatever micro-interpretations I may be inclined to extract from isolated texts. Each of the three—Father, Son, and Spirit—are playing their part by pointing to the other. It is, by definition, a three-person operation, each one selflessly deferring to the others. The moment we reduce the operation to the solo venture of a God who is defined as a solitary self, the entire story is drained of the relational dynamic of love and becomes a tale of divine narcissism.

Those who subscribe to the anti-Trinitarian perspective believe that (1) Christ was brought into existence by God the Father sometime long ago in eternity past, and that (2) the Holy Spirit is the emanating presence and/or power of Jesus and/or God the Father. However, with the single piece of deductive narrative logic we just considered, it is demonstrated, unequivocally, that the Holy Spirit is a personal being distinct from the Father and the Son. Here's the logic again from another angle:

Jesus repeatedly stated that His mission was to point to the Father. Every act and teaching of His ministry was meant to "glorify" the Father (John 12:28). As He came to the end of His ministry, Jesus prayed, "I have glorified You on the earth" (John 17:4). "He who has seen Me has seen the Father," He asserted (John 14:9).

The mission of the Holy Spirit is to point to Jesus. "He shall not speak of Himself," Jesus explained of the Holy Spirit's mission, but rather "He shall glorify Me" (John

16:13-14, KJV). "He shall not speak of himself . . . He shall clarify me" (Wycliffe Bible). "He won't draw attention to Himself . . . He will honor Me" (The Message).

And the Father points to Jesus, the three of them forming a ceaseless circle of humble, self-deferring love toward one another. "Behold! My Servant whom I uphold," the Father sings of Christ, "My Elect One in whom My soul delights!" (Isaiah 42:1). "This is My beloved Son, in whom I am well pleased," the Father announced at the baptism of Jesus (Matthew 3:17).

Here's the simple logic of the relational dynamic: if I point to someone, that act necessarily means I am not the someone to whom I point. The Holy Spirit cannot point to the Son, who points to the Father, and simultaneously *be* the Son or the Father. If the Holy Spirit *is* the Father glorifying the Father or the Son glorifying the Son, or the Father glorifying the Son who points to the Father, then neither the Father nor the Son is genuine in their profession of other-centered love. Their apparent humility in pointing away from themselves to the other is a sham. By erasing the distinct personhood of the Holy Spirit, the humility, and love of the relational dynamic vanishes, and we are left with a narcissistic God pointing to Himself. This is, of course, the core problem with the anti-Trinitarian doctrine: it portrays God in God's ultimacy as an absolute singularity, a solitary self, thus draining our conception of God of any meaningful idea of love.

The short version:

The Holy Spirit points to Jesus, who points to the Father. Therefore, the Holy Spirit is neither Jesus nor the Father.

In John 14:16, the same logic is evident:

> I will pray the Father, and He will give you another Helper (*parakletos*), that He may abide with you forever—the Spirit of truth. John 14:16-17

Notice:

- the Holy Spirit is sent,

- by the Father,

- in response to the prayer of Jesus.

There is nothing complicated, deep, or mysterious about this. We have before us the most basic of grammatical formulations. If the Holy Spirit is sent by the Father, at the request of Jesus, the Holy Spirit is not equivalent to either the Father or Jesus. Additionally, if the Holy Spirit is called "another Helper"—an-*other* in addition to Jesus—it is evident that the Holy Spirit is a personal being like Jesus, yet not Jesus, since the Holy Spirit comes to occupy the place vacated by Jesus. Only a person can meaningfully occupy the vacancy of a person. Leaving a microwave oven in my place as I depart from my children for a few days will not suffice. Their mother will do quite nicely, though. "Another Helper"—*parakletos*—basically means, *not me, but like me.* Jesus is a person, therefore the Holy Spirit is a person, like Jesus, but distinct from Jesus.

It really is that simple, and that crucial. Simple, because both the narrative and the grammar are straightforward. Crucial, because God is either a solitary self or a social unit, and the direction we go on this foundational point will determine the shape and tone of our entire theological system.

But simply proving, as a logical exercise, that the Holy Spirit is the third Person of the Godhead, is not sufficient. What we really need is to comprehend the super personal work that the third Person of the Godhead does in our super personal hearts. That's what we've done in this chapter, and the overall picture is truly wonderful.

In the biblical story, there are two human narratives to choose between: the narrative of the first Adam with its relational portfolio of dysfunction and death, and the narrative of the last Adam with its portfolio of covenant faithfulness and eternal life. The new birth occurs when a human being, born in the lineage of Adam, disavows the old man (Adam) and identifies with the new man (Christ). When a person chooses Christ over Adam, they are baptized to signify their new birth. And according to Jesus, baptism is to be conducted as a Trinitarian event:

All authority has been given to Me in heaven
and on earth. Go therefore and make disciples
of all the nations, baptizing them in the name
of the Father and of the Son and of the Holy
Spirit, teaching them to observe all things
that I have commanded you; and lo, I am with
you always, even to the end of the age. Amen.
Matthew 28:18-20

Jesus specifically instructed His followers to baptize
"in the name of the Father and of the Son and of the
Holy Spirit."

Why?

Well, because the love that exists between the Three
members of the Godhead is the very reality into which
Christ invites us.

While baptism has no saving power in and of itself, it is a
symbolic act that retells the story of Christ in miniature
and indicates my choice to enter into His story as my own.
And His story is one in which He has lived the perfect
life of covenantal love as a member of the human race,
died the covenant death for our sins, rose from the dead
victorious over death, and ascended to heaven as the
Son of God and our brother in the flesh, there to forever
enjoy unbroken fellowship with the Father and the Holy
Spirit. Baptism testifies that we have chosen the way of
covenantal love as our new mode of being.

So think this through very carefully: if God consists of the Father alone, with Jesus as a secondary God derived from the Father, and if the Holy Spirit is the emanating energy of the Father . . . watch this . . . the logic of baptism completely breaks down. The moment the relational dynamic between the Father, the Son, and the Holy Spirit is eliminated from our theological understanding—by depersonalizing the Holy Spirit and making Christ a generated being—the logic of baptism vanishes. The intimate love that exists between the Three coeternal Persons of the Godhead is the kind of life we are signifying through baptism. If that love is not ultimate to God's identity, the meaning of baptism is gone.

Love, not force, characterizes the ministry of the Holy Spirit. By virtue of the fact that God is infinitely more powerful than we are, communication from God to us must be conducted in a manner that does not override our freedom, in a way that allows for a love-motivated response. The Holy Spirit is constantly engaged, therefore, in a kind of appearing and disappearing act. In order for our covenant identity to be honored and cultivated, the Holy Spirit must necessarily be almost-but-not-quite absent from our mental processing. In order to communicate to us with maximum clarity while refraining from canceling out our freedom, the Holy Spirit must draw, but never force. As we give ourselves over to the personal internal communion of the Holy Spirit, we are gradually, incrementally cultivated toward responsible self-governance until, at last, love alone defines every

free act we perform. The Holy Spirit is, therefore, always
seeking communion with the human spirit in a revelatory
role that is nearly indistinguishable from our own
thought process. Like the air that constantly surrounds
and permeates us, the Holy Spirit is at once invisible
and impactful.

> The wind blows where it wishes, and you hear the
> sound of it, but cannot tell where it comes from
> and where it goes. So is everyone who is born of
> the Spirit. John 3:8

Really, anything more than that and we would be slaves
to an infinitely overpowering will. But by the gentle yet
persistent ministry of the Holy Spirit, we are not. The Holy
Spirit is the great *un*forcer of God's law, which is to say, the
Holy Spirit is the agent of the new covenant,

witnessing and wooing,

testifying and teaching,

convicting and communicating,

but never forcing.

"In becoming the Son of God, God bent reality itself, His reality, to meet us in our need."

CHAPTER TWENTY-ONE
A COVENANT STORY

As they say, whoever *they* are, "It is what it is, and it's not what it's not."

Profundity at its best.

Likewise, the Bible says what it says, and it doesn't say what it doesn't say.

The Sonship of Christ is a microcosm of Israel's Sonship history, plain and simple. This is what's going on in the biblical narrative. Astoundingly, while this is the singular vision of the prophets and apostles, it is completely missing from the non-Trinitarian literature. Reading the rather small spectrum of non-Trinitarian arguments, it is as if the Sonship narrative isn't even present in Scripture because it's not even acknowledged. I do not, however, believe the omission is intentional or nefarious on the part of non-Trinitarian advocates. I think it has, quite simply, totally eluded their notice.

But how can that be?

How can a theological system that is entirely focused on purporting to define what the Bible means by calling Jesus God's Son completely overlook the very point Scripture is making regarding the Sonship of Christ?

Well, the same way, as we say, a person can miss seeing the forest by focusing too exclusively on the trees. If you only ever stand up close to individual trees, all you'll see is individual trees. Only when you back up from the trees will you notice the breathtaking landscape the trees collectively compose. Likewise, we must pan out from individual verses of Scripture to take in the entire biblical landscape in order to notice that all the Sonship passages in the New Testament are derived from the Adamic, Abrahamic, Davidic Sonship story of the Old Testament. Proof-texting is the breeding ground of heresy, while the truth of Scripture belongs only to those who read, really read, the whole story.

If you try to interpret John 3:16, for example, in a narrative vacuum, you will almost inevitably come up with some kind of mysterious, metaphysical interpretation about a greater God giving birth to a lesser God sometime way back in the ancient eternal past. The prooftexting methodology has so trained us to *use* the Bible rather than *read* the Bible, that we don't easily see the whole of Scripture in one sweeping, coherent glance. We see verses from which to pick and choose in order to prove whatever theological agenda we happen to have, while Scripture itself it trying to tell us a big and beautiful story.

Once we read the whole Bible, all the anti-Trinitarian proof texts vanish in the light of the biblical narrative. As we have seen, none of the New Testament verses that speak of Jesus as God's Son have anything to do with Him being uniquely birthed from God sometime long ago in eternity past. This metaphysical narrative is nowhere found in Scripture. It is a philosophical fiction imposed upon the book.

All of the New Testament authors are telling the continuing story initiated by the Old Testament prophets. They knew that Adam was the original human son of God,

that Adam forfeited that Sonship position,

that God set in motion a plan to regain that position for humanity,

that God entered into covenant relation with Abraham to fulfill the plan,

that Isaac was Abraham's only begotten son of promise and therefore God's covenant son,

that Jacob was Isaac's firstborn son of promise and therefore the covenant son of God,

that Jacob's twelve sons became God's corporate covenant son as a nation called Israel,

that King David continued the Sonship succession and became God's covenant son,

and that David's son Solomon became God's covenant son in the ongoing lineage.

And knowing the Old Testament narrative, the New Testament writers knew that Jesus, born in this very lineage, was none other than the son of Abraham, the son of Israel, the son of David, and therefore the long-awaited covenant Son of God.

This is the story the Bible tells.

This is the story the New Testament writers understood Jesus to have fulfilled.

And this is, therefore, what they meant when they identified Jesus as the Son of God.

The Bible is not concerned with explaining to us the ontological origins or chronology of God.

It is, rather, a story of relational dynamics gone bad, and then made right again.

It is a covenant story, not a metaphysics philosophy.

To the question, "How long has God existed, and in what form?" God must just smile and say something like,

I have always existed for no length of time at all as you know time, and in no form whatsoever that you could possibly comprehend. So let's talk about something on your level. How 'bout I approach you as a Father so you can grasp how much I love you, and as a Son so you can know

that I am in deep solidarity with you, and as a Spirit so you can sense me communicating non-coercively within your spirit? I am more than your finite mind can imagine, but not less, so I'll show you everything you can comprehend in categories that will make sense to you in your context.

Because we are created, material beings, it is literally impossible for us to understand uncreated, non-material categories—namely, God. So God comes down to where we are.

Way down.

While we can never fully know *what* God is, we can know *who* God is. While we cannot know the *nature* of God, we can know the *character* of God. We can know how God thinks and feels and behaves. With ever-increasing clarity, we can know and experience God's love. We can run forever, full speed, into the light of His breathtaking beauty and never exhaust its infinite wealth.

But if we think we can explain *what* God is, it's not God we're talking about. If our conception of God is fully defined by the limited material categories of our own material, procreative, father-mother-son-daughter human reality, we haven't defined God, we've merely projected our image onto God. The truth of the matter is, God does not exist within the parameters of our little puddle of finite existence. We exist, as a droplet, within the infinite parameters of God's oceanic reality.

Jesus is the Son of God within the narrative plot line of Adam's creation and fall, then within the scope of Israel's prophetic history. Once we get our eyes fixed on the story being told in the Old Testament, the New Testament will make abundant and beautiful sense for the first time. The storyline of Scripture possesses all the explanatory power we need to make sense of the Sonship of Christ. Taking the Bible as a cohesive narrative with an overarching purpose, we have discovered what Scripture itself means by designating the Savior of the world as the Son of God. We don't need to guess. We barely even need to interpret. The story has told us what it wants us to know on the matter and has also left us with mystery regarding those things that are beyond our finite comprehension.

When John 3:16 calls Jesus God's "only begotten Son," the immediate context of the chapter needs to be carefully examined, within the larger context of John's Gospel as a whole, within the even larger context of John's source material, which is the entire Old Testament narrative. We have done just that in our journey, and we now *know* what the Bible means when it speaks of Jesus as God's "only begotten Son."

When the apostle Paul calls Jesus God's "firstborn" Son, this language does not merely occur in single, isolated Pauline verses, but rather within the context of a line of thinking Paul is developing within the whole book of Romans, which Paul is basing on the much larger context of the big story unfolded in the Old Testament regarding a succession of "firstborn" sons that would lead up to the Messiah. We looked at that material, and we now *know* what the Bible itself means when it uses the word "firstborn" to describe Jesus.

We *know* what the Sonship of Christ means because we've taken the whole story of Scripture into account, not merely a selection of detached verses. And what it means is quite astounding.

God is a God of faithful, unfailing, steadfast, covenantal love, and we were made to live in reciprocal, covenantal relationship with God and one another. In the final analysis, the most coherent thing we can say about God is that "God is love." And that's a lot to say. It was this reality that led God to reach out of Himself to become a member of the human race. God so deeply, passionately, selflessly loves the human race, that He chose to enter into eternal solidarity with us as our Brother in the flesh. The Creator of the universe—the God who engineered the intricate details of life in all its forms—voluntarily became one with us in order to restore us to oneness with Himself.

In becoming the Son of God, God bent reality itself, His reality, to meet us in our need.

God did this for you.

For me.

He became what He was not so that we could become all we're meant to be.

This is the story of the Bible, and it's nothing short of the best story imaginable, because it's a covenant story . . .

and that means it's a love story.